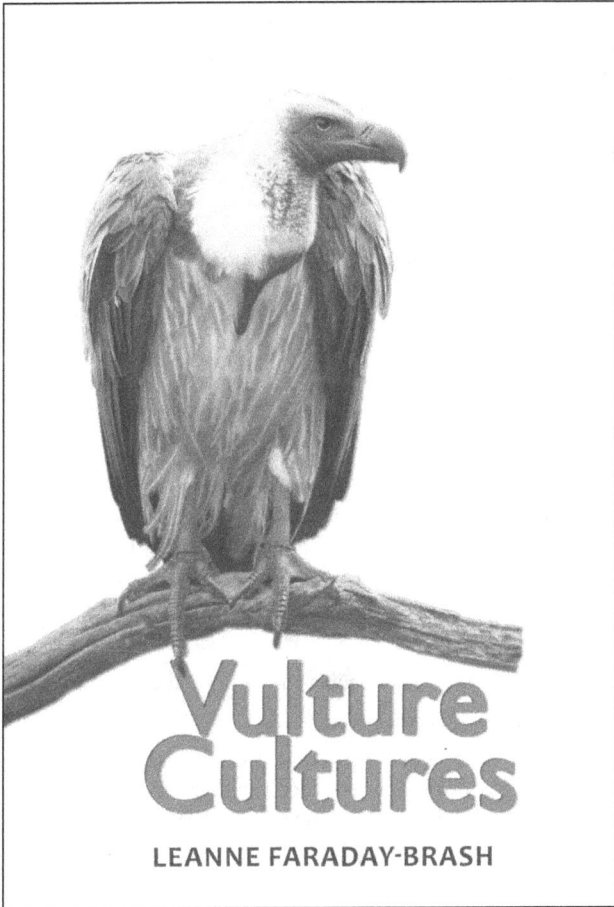

Vulture Cultures

LEANNE FARADAY-BRASH

AUSTRALIANACADEMIC**PRESS**

First published in November 2012
Australian Academic Press
Level 5, Toowong Tower,
9 Sherwood Road,
Toowong QLD 4066, Australia
www.australianacademicpress.com.au

National Library of Australia Cataloguing-in-Publication entry:

Author:	Faraday-Brash, Leanne.
Title:	Vulture cultures : how to stop them ravaging your organisation's performance, people, profit and public image / Leanne Faraday-Brash.
ISBN:	9781922117038 (pbk.) 9781922117045 (ebook)
Subjects:	Work environment--Psychological aspects. Organizational behavior. Personnel management. Psychology, Industrial.

Dewey Number: 658.3045

Book and cover design by Maria Biaggini — The Letter Tree.
Image by ©istockphoto/Michael Zirkler.

Most businesses and organisations are now realising the importance of culture in achieving organisational objectives. And yet there are far too many examples of poor company cultures in which staff are not engaged.

Leanne takes a subject that is confronting and challenging to most and makes it understandable and manageable. Avoiding jargon while balancing theory with plenty of examples to which readers at all levels of experience can relate, 'Vulture Cultures' makes the topic of organisational culture accessible to anyone.

Consistent with her teaching and consulting style, Leanne covers a wide range of topics across this critical subject with insight and advice you can really implement. 'Vulture Cultures' is a must read for any leader in just about any type of organisation. I highly recommend this book!

— *Mark Stoermer, Director Corporate Services, City of Melbourne*

I love this book. Leanne is a gifted writer and the knowledge and the stories she shares are so powerful. A must read for every leader who wants to shape a better culture.

— *Dimitra Manis, Senior Vice President,*
Global Head of People, Thomson Reuters

This is an outstanding contribution to the solution of an age old problem; the effects of bullying and bad leadership in the workplace. It is not difficult to recognise many of the characters that Leanne portrays but what is often forgotten is the extreme detrimental effect that they have on the organisations with which they are involved and not uncommonly lead. Anyone who has worked in organisations where these people hold leadership positions will cringe in sympathy for their unfortunate subordinates. Perhaps even some of those portrayed will recognise themselves and seek to mend their ways. A timely and sensible contribution.

— *Alastair Nicholson AO RFD QC, Former Chief Justice,*
Chair of the National Centre Against Bullying

To those wonderful leaders who know their people deserve the chance to flourish at work

Acknowledgments

knew I wanted to write this book for some three years now. With a busy consulting practice and children to raise, it rightfully took a back seat in my head for a while. However with all the scandals coming out of the Global Financial Crisis, the industrial disputes and front page sexual harassment cases, the tragic suicide of a young Victorian woman who was bullied at her place of work and the despair felt by so many in workplaces starved of empathy and vision, I decided I had to make it a priority.

I thank those of you who implored me to write it and for those who offered to be interviewed. I hope those who believe they are currently denied their right to flourish at work, see improvements over time. I am hopeful the so-called Generation Y will experience more visionary, supportive and egalitarian leadership than previous generations and that the phenomenon that is positive psychology will sow seeds that will take root and cultivate happier, healthier workplaces.

Thank you to my clients who entrust me with their most embarrassing and painful workplace secrets, knowing I won't judge them. The life of a consultant is a privilege, the chance to sit with a leader one coaches, a gift. The chance to play even the smallest part in the growth of others who participate in our training courses is a wondrous thing. I never grow tired of it.

To Stephen May of Australian Academic Press who was excited by the concept in its most formative stages, thank you for your faith and professionalism. To Maria Biaggini, thank you for your warmth and enthusiasm, for listening to what I wanted and for the fabulous work you did on book and cover design. I'd like to extend a special thank you to my US editor who collaborated on this project from the other side of the world, Kristin Walinski. Thanks also to my website designer, social media guru, friend and consultant I have dubbed 'the bossy publicist', Melissa Bickford from Artisan Media.

To my parents, husband, children and siblings, thank you for your love and strength. My work sometimes takes a lot out of me and that doesn't always mean there's a lot left.

And finally a sincere thank you to my colleagues; that tribe of trainers, consultants, facilitators and professional speakers who have become my dear friends and make me want to be better and do better every day.

Leanne Faraday–Brash
September 2012

Contents

Contents (CONT.)

PART ONE

'Vultures Nesting, Culture Testing'

Chapter 1

Behind this Book

Everyone has a personality. When you hear comments about the person who allegedly has 'no personality', it's not true. You may find some people dull and expressionless but I promise you, they still have a personality. It may not be extroverted, inspiring, quirky, expressive, or appealing to you — but everyone has a personality.

And so it is with organisations and parts thereof: they also have a personality. But when we talk about groups of people we use the word 'culture' instead of personality. There are complex definitions of 'culture' but for our purposes, are they so helpful? Organisational consultants Terrence Deal and Allan Kennedy defined culture as 'the way things are done around here'. Note that the definition goes to the way things are *done* — **not** to what we *say* is important, how we *say* we do things, or what we *say* we stand for — but how we really *do* things.

When I was in my late twenties with two small children, my husband found an advertisement in the paper for a job he said sounded tailor-made for me. The chance to branch out at that time of my life and spend time with individuals whose mean age was greater than three sounded exciting! It was a senior consulting role with a large Australian bank based in a beautiful inner-city suburb, with lots of scope for professional development and interesting work.

I applied, had a conniption about childcare when I was offered the role, and started work four weeks later. I remember three things about my first day: the surreal experience of being able to make myself a coffee whenever I wanted, the opportunity to go to the bathroom without toddlers who insisted on keeping me company, and the sage advice a generous colleague gave me. 'Okay, Leanne. Has anyone told you the 'Billy Bloggs' rule?' When I informed my colleague no one had, she proceeded to share. 'I'm not exactly sure what your core hours are and whether you are an early or late starter and finisher, but the general rule of thumb is this: If you leave work before 6 p.m., leave via the southeast corner door. If you leave after 6 p.m., be sure to walk past Billy's office, say 'good night' so he notices you, and leave via the door nearest reception'. I learnt quickly that face time was important and that part-timers weren't accorded the same opportunities as their full-time counterparts.

And things soon changed for the worse. When my inspirational boss resigned, a new chief manager fresh from twenty years with a chartered accounting firm replaced her. He called the women working in leadership and development 'The Hen's Club'. Yet the bank began to tout its progressiveness with examples of extraordinarily 'enlightened' practices such as part-time female senior managers and talked up their impressive track record of women at the chief manager level. When you asked someone about these special women, you discovered that actually there were only a handful. And within a year, they had all resigned and gone elsewhere. This gives you a flavour of the prevailing aspects of the culture.

Despite that, the job had other redeeming features such as relaxed, autonomous leadership from my immediate boss and the scope to do cutting-edge work, thanks mostly to the influence of my aforementioned inspirational, transformational boss. So I stayed for six years, had two more babies in between, and went out on my own, never to return to salaried employment again.

This book is not however a chest-beating book about gender discrimination and culture that is inhospitable to any workgroup, female or otherwise. It is a book that identifies a number of attributes of destructive workplace cultures, encourages an honest appraisal, and proffers advice on how to improve culture to enhance opportunities for the gregarious and the introverted as well as men, women, baby boomers, Gen Y's and so forth. In other words, its goal is to enable *anyone* to survive and thrive in a culture that is safe and inclusive yet drives performance, profit, innovation, and talent retention. With a healthy culture as an important goal, a source of competitive advantage, and an explicit strategic imperative, the employee wins, but so does the company. Destructive behaviours are classified as *vulturesque* because they are any or all of unethical, illegal, or otherwise counterproductive.

I have worked as an independent consultant long enough to value the importance of realism. This book does not assume that an organisation's primary raison d'être is to serve its people, but it does assume the moral and legal imperative to look after its people whilst pursuing its strategic business goals. My daily ambition as a consultant is to help clients understand that great people management is not just a means to an end but a wonderful way to catalyse engagement, productivity, and innovation. Who can be motivated and creative when their fundamental needs aren't met?

The Underlying Assumptions of This Book

This book is based on the following premises:

1. **It is not enough to pay people a salary for turning up to work.** Many moral and legal obligations are associated with the support of the employees in our care. Buying into this

premise is imperative if you want to change the culture. Employees get paid to do a job. Being inspired and enriched might seem like attractive added extras. Being bullied, subjugated, demeaned, manipulated, cheated, disadvantaged unlawfully, or led by incompetents are not.

2. **Good culture, in and of itself, will not guarantee individual and organisational performance.** Other factors can compromise success even if it's a 'great place to work'. Having said that, a growing body of evidence suggests that good culture, compassionate leadership, and happy people in organisations create a competitive advantage. Furthermore, new evidence suggests the ability to show appreciation — one attribute of attractive leadership — is intrinsic to true happiness.

3. **'Bad' cultures can be 'successful', according to some criteria such as profitability and shareholder return.** Some organisations have terrible reputations for the way they treat staff, vendors, and customers yet make a lot of money, particularly if they have something everyone wants that not many people supply. Yes, they can succeed in the absence of real competition, at least for a while. But listen to the way people talk about them and the lengths to which a resentful customer can be willing to go to find an alternative supplier. People are more likely to rely on what others say about an organisation than what it says about itself, and a bad reputation is only a few keystrokes away on a Google search. In an era where disgruntled customers or ex-employees can set up websites dedicated to flaming you or send an instantaneous tweet into the *twitterverse*, bad behaviour cannot be taken lightly. It hurts business.

4. **Some people will be content to, or at least prepared to, work in bad cultures.** I make no simplistic threat that we will automatically lose our best and brightest because of a toxic work environment (especially if some of our best and brightest are the ones contributing to the toxicity). Why might they get away with it, you ask? Some of them deliver, so

the organisation sacrifices culture for performance. Those who don't perpetrate but stay and suffer may have chained themselves to the organisational treadmill via discounted loans and lucrative benefits or conditions. They may be financially vulnerable or apprehensive about entering the job market, and the devil they know seems preferable. They may be extremely well remunerated or enjoy other aspects of the work (e.g., high autonomy) that, in their minds, balance out the equation. They may be able to objectify the bad or unethical behaviour as separate from them and display above-average resilience. However, some staff will feel victimised or compromised by the prevailing culture and will not fare so well. The lack of choice, or the perception of a lack of choice, and the ensuing feelings of entrapment contribute substantially to illness and depression as well as change resistance.

5. **Every person who works in a company is a custodian of the company's culture, but some will have more impact than others.** Each of us interacts with, behaves, makes decisions, and has some control over something or someone, so each of us helps shape the place where we work. That is not to say workplaces are equitable. Many of us know the famous quote from George Orwell's classic, *Animal Farm*: 'All animals are equal, but some are more equal than others'. And as Captain Ramsey said in *Crimson Tide*: 'We're here to preserve democracy, not practise it'.

In a system (e.g., team, department, or company), everyone influences the system, but some will have more reach than others. Again, context is key here. We have the capacity to disrupt the system by performing one action that is different from what we did yesterday (also known as the Butterfly Effect) and create the potential for a different reaction. For those reading this book who are seriously senior and carry real clout, you can make the biggest difference to others and to the system.

6. **The insights shared here and the theories and strategies enunciated here are *portable*.** While this is ostensibly a business book, families have cultures also. I would be lying, as a proud mother of four, if I did not say I care deeply about raising children in a safe environment where they are given the best chance to reach their potential as human beings and as members of their system. Thus, I am hoping the opinions and insights shared here, and those sparked as you read, will migrate to other parts of your life.

7. **This book needs to offer practical advice to be effective.** I want to make sure I provide you with some useful assistance. I will not shy away from a good concept or model, but I will also ask you some down-to-earth focus questions that you can't run and hide from. I will be direct at times, but that is not a gratuitous attempt to shock or unhinge for the sake of it. I will tell stories, and I may make you uncomfortable, but it will be up to you to decide whether some good can come from your insights. While you read, I hope we will be having a conversation. Remember, things will only change if you do *something*. Awareness is the necessary first step.

8. **Beyond those already mentioned, the one overarching premise of this book is that one way or another, bad culture *costs* — possibly *big time!***

The Double-Edged Sword of Leadership

If you're a CEO or a general manager, your people watch you. Leadership is like parenting: your children learn from you when you want them to, and they learn from you when you don't. You can't just turn to staff on any given day and say, 'Hey, I'm not feeling really credible and emotionally intelligent today. Could you just please follow someone else while I go into a cupboard and scream into a pillow?'

What you *do* carries more weight. Therefore, if you behave badly, it has more gravitas. There is also more permission around it. You tend to have more freedom, choice, and pull than anyone else in the organisation, but you also have to carry the most responsibility.

If many staff are honest, they want to *be you* or *be liked by you*, the psychoanalytic parent figure, so they will do what they need to do to please you (feeding their aspirational drive) or guard against abandonment or rejection by you (harnessing their protective drive).

Plus if *you're* in charge and let *them* get away with bad behaviour, even if you don't perpetrate it yourself, then you're saying it's acceptable behaviour. That may serve as classical conditioning for the behaviour to be repeated, especially if the behaviour invokes positive consequences.

I'm all for businesses making money, so I am not suggesting we head up organisations with save-the-world types. Firstly, history has shown they're not commercially minded, so they're unlikely to get themselves employed too often. With a small handful born in every generation, there are not enough to occupy the number of CEO positions going round anyway. Just as importantly, in large, complex, and diffuse organisations, one person is not going to do the job that needs to be done, so we will leave the Mahatma Gandhis of this world to advocate passionately around global issues of poverty, hunger, and peace. The rest of us mere mortals can concentrate on making a dent in what's dysfunctional or dastardly, on what's unintended but possibly unethical, and on destructive conflict and divisiveness at work because they *cost*.

Good culture and performance do not automatically go together, nor are they mutually exclusive. I have worked with highly profitable organisations that drive their people very hard and have ugly reputations but high engagement. Some companies pride themselves on their ability to look after their people, yet settle for mediocrity as people take advantage of soft or absent leadership; becoming spoilt, entitled, and motivated entirely by self-interest. However, one assertion of this book is that the leaders of an organisation are the custodians of its culture and may have to make gutsy decisions in the name of culture and ethics that, at least initially, fly in the face of business interests.

Anyway, that's enough about me. Let's talk about you.

Reasons to Read This Book

1. You're curious about cultures so dysfunctional that they bear no resemblance to your own but you want to know how the other half live. If so, then enjoy the read and celebrate what you have.

2. You have a sneaking suspicion that not everything about where you work is magical, and you want to see whether you can recognise any villains in our story and learn how to handle them. Read on; you'll undoubtedly find some if you have more than ten people in your organisation.

3. You know you work in a cesspool of misery, and this book may help galvanise you to do something about it. The book will come with no magic wand or bulletproof vest, and I am not arrogant enough to suggest my models and strategies are foolproof, but they may help you find the gumption and a plan of action to improve your situation.

4. You are a leader or very senior leader in an organisation looking for some answers to what you suspect or know is happening on your watch. It is your moral, ethical, and legal responsibility to do something about this for the sake of your business and its shareholders, clients, and staff. Read on; if some of the stories I tell you here read like your autobiography, I can promise you they will be costing someone big time!

It may not always be comfortable or easy to find solutions to the problems of a vulture culture, but culture can be changed. Some simple cause-and-effect principles can make a profound difference. In any case, recognise that by preserving the status quo, you have made a default choice, and you bear no less responsibility except that you don't yet have the accompanying focus, plan, and strategy to improve anything. And that's a scary place to be. In the immortal words of Robert King 'Bob' Steele, former Under Secretary for Domestic Finance of the US Treasury, 'Hope is not a strategy'.

Therefore, in summary, this book is for any employee and every change leader in organisations big and small who wants to actively shape a better culture — one that makes your workplace a great place to work. If you are a big fish, you can make a big difference. If you are a small fish, you will want to look after yourself and those around you.

We are all custodians of culture, and every transaction we have with people perpetuates or shifts workplace culture.

Maintaining Perspective

All of us have a natural yearning to understand others and ourselves. We are all psychologists of life. Thus there needs to be some reference in this book to psychological and interpersonal constructs and concepts to make sense of what creates and perpetuates good and bad cultures, without talking too much *psychobabble*. Thus, I will not shy away from a discussion on cognitive dissonance, intent vs. impact, family systems, and the importance of context and early life experiences (including our 'inner child' with 'unmet needs') in making sense of culture and work behaviours. However, I won't throw around words like 'psychopath' and 'sociopath' in a way that implies everyone who's a bit moody at work is a candidate for the label. Nor will I assume that if you find a person difficult or even toxic, everyone will. A relationship is a dynamic interaction. If you are pushing each other's buttons, it's a system involving two or more people that creates that situation.

An Important Note — Let's Talk!

If you connect profoundly with any of the stories or case studies in the book and need to discuss them, and a friend, a coach, or a journal won't suffice, then I would be thrilled to chat with you. The use of e-mail and social media, including blogging and LinkedIn, seem the perfect ways to begin these conversations.

You can find me at www.brashconsulting.com.au or www.vulturecultures.com.

You can connect with me on LinkedIn or email me directly at lfb@vulturecultures.com.

The Format of this Book

Part One begins with a definition of vulture cultures and the risks and costs associated with bad organisational behaviour. It examines the reasons vulture cultures are created and perpetuated against all good common sense. The last chapter of Part One is a Warning Signs and Risk Factors Inventory that enables you to do some honest and private reflection on the current health of your workplace and the quality of your working life.

Part Two is devoted to an exploration of the various types of vulture cultures. That is, it chronicles the types of destructive behaviours and provides rich case examples of real-life occurrences in the public domain and in my consulting practice that were sadly memorable for the lost productivity, reduced profitability, deep dysfunction, and emotional stress for individual employees over the two decades I have been consulting.

Part Three is devoted to strategies with an emphasis on how senior leaders and organisations can shift culture to the positive despite resistance, fear, and the battered mentality of staff who have lost hope or confidence that things can be different. These successful strategies are borne out of countless interventions I have run over many years and document what helps sincere organisations arrest the harm and pave the way for something better for their people. The last chapter of Part Three is devoted to supporting individuals, as I never want them to feel alone or more isolated than they do now.

Confidentiality — Protecting the Innocent and the Downright Guilty

Some of the case examples used in the book are drawn from well publicised events that have been extensively covered in the media. In these cases, I am talking about real people and corporations, and therefore I use real names and businesses. I should point out that the opinions expressed in every instance are my own, unless otherwise indicated.

In other cases, the stories are based on teams and organisations that I have consulted and individuals I have worked with closely. While at times, I may disclose the sector in which these companies operated, the names of individuals and their titles are fictitious so that all these people and companies remain anonymous.

I have liberally included descriptions of various types of *vulturesque* behaviour I have encountered many times over in organisations I have worked with. Regrettably, none of the details of these situations have been embellished or dramatised to make for more compelling reading. This is what I have seen, and the strategies we have put in place and the outcomes we have achieved are real and continue to be effective. I say effective because we see people motivated to make their workplaces healthier, happier, and more productive, and their leadership is genuinely committed to doing the hard yards to make this happen.

Happy reading!

Chapter 2

Why Vulture Cultures?

Numerous corporate scandals exploding across the US, UK and Europe over the years leading into and post the global financial crisis have revealed work cultures rife with mismanagement and dysfunctional. Having said that, while my predominant professional consulting experience has been in Australia, many of the same themes reverberate here across corporate and government. Thus, the vulture may be indigenous to North America (as well as Africa and Asia), but the inclination to prey on the weak and the vulnerable; the uncanny ability to swoop on, claw, and tear at good culture and ethics; and the flow-on negative consequences for innovation, engagement, health, well-being, and productivity know no international borders.

Here's a quick refresher on collective nouns:

- A group of lions is a pride.
- A group of cattle is a herd.
- A group of geese is a gaggle.
- A group of seagulls is a flock.
- A group of vultures is ... a committee! (Yes, really!)

Rarely does one vulture act alone. Vultures either roam in packs, or the head vulture wreaks havoc whilst those in the committee around them enable, apologise, pathologise, hide, obfuscate, rationalise, deflect, and ultimately normalise the behaviour. They either:

1. Actively practise or adopt the behaviour over time,

2. Condone the behaviour (directly or indirectly), or

3. Pay no heed to what's happening on their watch and are duplicitous via negligence.

In the first two situations, they know what is going on and allow it to continue, almost always out of fear: fear they won't get what they want or fear that if they push back, they'll get something they don't want or will lose something they have that's valuable. Thus, greed may motivate, but so might the threat of diminished power or status.

In the third, ignorance is bliss. However, it is also negligent and immoral if destructive behaviour and the creation and maintenance of a destructive workplace culture happens under their noses because they don't read the warning signs or fail to ask the right questions. And why might they fail to ask the questions? We come full circle to a discussion of fear again. They may not ask the questions because they don't want to hear the answers. Once they do, they may feel compelled to do something or know they'll get into trouble if they don't. I've watched enough episodes of the television series *West Wing* and *24*, to see that plausible deniability seems quite handy at times. Thus, in simple terms, fear and destructive behaviour go hand in hand. If the perpetrator isn't acting out of fear, she may be getting away with a lot because the person on the receiving end of this behaviour is fearful.

Therefore, it would seem obvious that one of the keys to a great work culture is to stamp out fear. Indeed, much of my argument about effective strategies is about making it safe for people to speak up and be accountable. Though Jamie Lee Curtis's character in the movie *True Lies* famously declares, 'Fear is not an option', well, sorry, it is.

In a detailed discussion in Part Three about strategies, we will see that there is one healthy fear in organisations: the fear — or the belief — that if I do the wrong thing, I will experience negative consequences. Deterrence is a primitive and straightforward logic, but fight/flight serves a purpose, as does drinking when we're thirsty. Sometimes the exquisitely simple works the best. Not everything that's good for us has to be complicated. The fear of disciplinary action or dismissal, reputational risk, and prosecution are perfectly legitimate levers to pull. However, they are a far cry from doing the right thing because it's the right thing to do. The best cultures work both ends of the continuum.

One person doesn't constitute a culture, but one person in a system may engage in toxic behaviour. Culture is created and maintained by a collective. Therefore, we do not assume here that a vulture culture is one in which several or all members of the system must be behaving badly, but they are all contributing to the perpetuation of the toxicity in direct or indirect ways. And while one person doesn't create a culture, a bad culture can have a profound impact on one person, even after a 'toxic' person is removed. Not only might the victim be a casualty of a war, but the behaviour and the ensuing response (or lack thereof) to what's happened can also have dramatic ramifications over time for the larger organisation. Every time an individual brings a destructive or debilitating act on another and those in the organisation who could do something about it support, condone, ignore, or fail to detect the act, it *weakens* the culture.

With that premise, let's take the examples below of employees working in a dysfunctional culture and consider the act of one or more against one and the impact on many.

The Example of One(s)

Meet Ben

He's excited to have been selected in his first full-time job out of university. He takes a job as a graduate in state government. He hopes to encounter a dynamic, intelligent workplace and thrive there. Instead, he walks into a demoralized, punitive culture where young people are told implicitly and explicitly to know their place. The fresh graduates are treated like cannon fodder; most become burnt out and disillusioned within a year. They know they deserve better, but they've been beaten about the head since they got there for being too big for their boots, too ambitious, and merely 'good at passing exams with no clue about the real world'. Ben feels the focus and enthusiasm he had since he started dissipate at an alarming rate, so he applies for six months unpaid leave to travel after a year, with no real thought to return. He comes home from his trip and takes a job with a nonprofit organisation where he is intensely happy. He resolves never to work for a baby boomer and never to work in government again. His entire view of that world has been tainted by his early experience.

Meet Beryl

She has worked for the same organisation for twenty-three years and as a personal assistant for her managing director for twelve years. She is loyal and committed, if only slightly resistant to the uptake of technology. However, with encouragement, intensive training, and support, she's slowly gotten there. She is proud of her role in supporting the executive and protectively guards the gate without being obstructive or belligerent, ensuring his time is safeguarded against irrelevancies and impulse. She is an institution and fondly thought of. Her boss retires and is replaced by a more driven and insensitive manager who is intent on changing everything in the place in five minutes, including Beryl. Beryl believes the new manager has done everything in his power to make life difficult for her in the hope she will just make life easy and retire. The new manager frequently vents frustration at Beryl without ever having given clear direction, berates her in front of other executives, and has made her so stressed she is not performing at the top of her game. She is not sleeping and is often teary. Following an altercation with her boss where the boss tells Beryl the relationship is not working out, the boss appoints another personal assistant (twenty years younger and quite officious). Beryl puts in a work cover claim citing stress, has been off work for eight weeks, and can't find the intestinal fortitude to go back to work, having lost face and feeling humiliated. In her first few weeks of absence, she receives a few sporadic phone calls from staff who are genuinely concerned for her but ask her not to tell anyone they have been in contact. The calls are decreasing in frequency, and Beryl feels the team has moved on without her. Beryl is broken-hearted to think a forty-year career may have ended in this way.

Meet Bill

Bill has worked in the police force as a uniformed member and undercover cop for twelve years. He has always stayed on the straight and narrow. His worst offense was to inadvertently and occasionally take home a notepad (not that this wouldn't technically constitute petty theft). After transferring into a different unit, Bill is shocked at the looseness he encounters in relationships between criminals and police: specifically, the degree of fraternisation, the way in which people seem to turn a blind eye to certain things that go on, and reports and documents that should have been but weren't written. He feels incapable of saying anything as they all seem to be in on it. From what he can gather, not everyone participates in these things, but a culture of condoning makes him feel compromised. On one occasion, he plucks up the courage to ask a fellow team member about a questionable work practice, receives a look of derision, and is told: 'You've been here five minutes. It's not for you to judge'.

He asks for a transfer eight months in but can't bring himself to tell anyone why he's asked to get out except that it 'just isn't a good fit'. He is still nervy about the possibility that someone he worked with will try to maintain he was in on things because he didn't stand up against them. He still feels down on himself for not being willing to do anything proactive to change the culture. His self-esteem has suffered, he believes he's blotted his copybook, and he is at a loss to explain why he felt so vulnerable in that environment.

Meet Carly

She has lunch on her own every day. She was recruited by a boss with a major change agenda to deliver. The department had not been travelling well. Staff are insecure and have been allowed to behave badly for a long time. Carly is bright and enthusiastic. With no allegiance to the past and a good appetite for change, she makes the fatal mistake of voicing her early support for the manager and the change. She struggles to establish relationships within the team: some withhold information, which slows her down or embarrasses her, and she has gone in a short period from being a confident, capable person to feeling alienated and isolated. The unspoken rule seems to be 'You're either with me or against me', and the rest of the department decides that she is with the manager and against them.

She previously prided herself on her ability to establish rapport. She knows she is a team player, but can't easily crack this group of resisters. She decides to get some help when she wakes up one Monday morning and has a full-blown panic attack at the thought of going to work. She accesses the Employee Assistance Program (confidential company counselling service) and is working on some strategies to become more assertive and call the behaviour when she feels she is being harassed or frozen out. The counsellor suggests she take time away from the workplace, but Carly thinks that means the others will have won. She also knows that the work won't get done and worries she'll appear pathetic to her new boss.

In Ben's case, the arrogance of older workers, whether born of insecurity or ignorance, creates a hostile work environment for young, intelligent staff who have enough of a sense of their own self-worth and the freedom and courage to go elsewhere. Thus, a potentially talented, bright staff member is lost to the organisation and forms the same prejudiced ideas that created his alienation in the first place.

Beryl was a loyal and effective servant of the organisation for decades. It took only a few months for Beryl to have a crisis of confidence and experience major physical and psychological health symptoms because a new manager, with no empathy and homage to the past, rode roughshod over her feelings, compelling her to find a way out and finish work in very ignominious fashion. Not only is this a tragedy for Beryl, but while she is not around to witness it, what of the disillusionment, rage, or disappointment for other members of the team seeing Beryl treated shabbily? And what about the lost opportunity for Beryl to have left on her terms but only after she had shared some of her tremendous local knowledge with the organisation prior to her departure? Everyone loses, even the silly boss who thinks he's won: by having a personal assistant he chose but who's created anxiety and insecurity in the new staff. Because of the treatment doled out to Beryl, he has sent a subliminal message about the way things are going to be now that he's here.

Bill's mistake appears to have been an unwillingness to conform to the unspoken norms of that group. Moreover, he would have appeared judgmental and disapproving, and no one likes people to hold up a mirror and make it clear they don't like what they see. There is room in some organisations for significant quirkiness and individuality, so long as you don't stand out on the stuff that really counts! (For a study of eccentricity, see the book *Crazy Bosses*.)

In Carly's case, the exclusion and disapproval of her for being willing to come to work to be happy and positive about the future (obviously, that was considered highly offensive) was enough to put her off side with a powerful clique at work who held the balance of power. This vulture culture did not prey on the weak or vulnerable, but it was able to make her feel that way over time. Carly was victimised because the existing culture was unhealthy and antagonistic. Building a positive relationship with an enthusiastic new staff member was tantamount to fraternising with the enemy.

Whilst the examples above are stories of individuals, the same causes and effects can be seen in teams, branches, departments, and indeed whole organisations. Even when counterproductive workplace behaviour — whether unlawful, unethical, or otherwise dysfunctional — occurs in a discrete patch, the impact of such culture and the behaviours it produces can be felt in other parts of the organisation and accompanied by disastrous consequences.

Case Study — News of the World by Murdoch Publications

At the time of writing this book, a British tabloid newspaper, *News of the World*, a British institution first published 167 years ago and owned by Rupert Murdoch's global media firm News Limited, was accused of having allegedly tapped the phones of family members of people who had been murdered, including soldiers killed in Afghanistan and others. The vast majority of the 200 or so journalists working for the paper probably had nothing to do with such despicable acts of gutter journalism. But the widely held view was that the editor at the time these acts were being perpetrated, Rebekah Brooks, would have known about them at the very least, and so would her deputies.

So how did News International, the parent organisation, respond to these allegations? It announced on 7 July 2011 that it was shutting down the entire paper. The last edition ran on Sunday 10 July with a simple front page that said 'Thank You and Good Bye'. Yet some commentators have suggested that the closure had more to do with shoring up the company's chance of a favourable decision on a $10 billion broadcasting deal for Channel B Sky B than righting a wrong. Maybe the bad guys won. Most staff lost their jobs, hapless victims of what seemed a particularly ruthless business decision. After all, there was no suggestion that a majority of the paper's staff were involved in illegal activities.

The scandal was deemed so newsworthy that it inspired a major storyline in Aaron Sorkin's brilliant television show *The Newsroom*. Bad culture costs. It costs individuals, teams, and organisations. Good culture on its own won't guarantee performance and profits, but bad culture will almost certainly prevent an organisation from reaching its potential and being admired in the marketplace.

One individual does not make a culture, but a system that condones, rationalises, or protects that individual is, or has the potential to be, a vulture culture.

Chapter 3

The Why and How of Vultures Nesting

With so many obvious impacts on individuals, engagement, morale, talent retention, and reputation, we need to figure out how vulture cultures happen and why they continue to happen.

The Power of the Peer Group

It is a fascinating yet sometimes treacherous indictment of us as a species that we tend to adopt the dominant behaviours of those around us. The good news is we are educable, which also means we are malleable. Sociologists call it *homosocial reproduction* — we become what we are surrounded by. Colloquially put, we adopt the behaviours of those we hang out with.

For those of us who experience a profound values clash with people we work for, and assuming the job market is not disastrous and we have some self-belief, we will probably get up and leave if we can't reconcile where we want to be with where we are. However, if we decide to stay for any number of reasons, how do we reconcile who we are with where we are? Some people with high emotional intelligence can externalise the behaviour, see it for what it is, and insulate against personal damage. In some cases, we insulate ourselves by adopting avoidance or protection strategies. In other cases, we find like-minded individuals and become our own posse. In that case, we will often witness two or more camps or tribes in the workplace: those who do and those who don't. Yet another strategy to manage the discomfort of that values clash is to subconsciously adopt the mantra of the pack mentality — if you can't beat them, join them.

Psychologist Evelyn Field summarises this beautifully in the context of one of the dominant forms of vulturesque behaviour, bullying:

> *Thus the average nice person is affected by where they are, not who they are. Most human beings are social animals who follow their tribe. Like the members of a cult, few people have the courage to defy a tyrant. Thus employees behave with respect and empathy in a healthy workplace and become offensive or defensive in a dysfunctional one. Then anyone can be targeted or bully, the climate can change, compliance becomes compulsory, dictators are created and emulated, and minor negative behaviours escalate into major harm. (Field, 2010, 'Bully Blocking at Work: A Self-Help Guide for Employees and Managers', p. 22).*

While the serial bad behaver may deny, justify, defend, and blame, the rest of us may not. It's unlikely to lead to behaviour change in the other party, and it does not usually make us feel any better. However, knowledge can empower us. If we understand better, we can mindfully observe our reactions and purposefully change our responses. This is one reason why we document some of the behaviours that typify vulture cultures in this book. Even if it is not necessarily helpful or accurate to pathologise this behaviour, we can't afford to normalise it, either.

Some other factors that can catalyse and perpetuate vulturesque behaviour include:

- personality attributes,
- existing cultural norms (poor legacy culture),
- existence of, and intolerance of, difference,
- poor or absent work systems,
- poor role clarity,
- high job insecurity or job stress,
- learnt behaviour like that we have seen in families of origin, and
- learnt behaviour that may actively be incentivised, rewarded, or lauded at work such as that we have seen feature prominently in the media, politics, corporate and banking.

Most subversive of all, we sometimes actively select for such behaviours because we frame them as positive qualities such as 'results oriented', 'focussed', 'driven', 'ambitious', and 'committed'.

Recruitment and Job-Related Selection Criteria

Unless we are an organisation of one, typically we get appointed. Organisations can actively select for job criteria that may have a positive or negative impact on other people and on culture. Mitchell Kusy and Elizabeth Holloway's research in their book *Toxic Workplace!* points to the idea that high doses of *congeniality* and *agreeableness* predict inversely for toxicity; thus, if we select for those two qualities, we are less likely to have to deal with the fallout of counterproductive work behaviour.

Not every organisation will have the financial resources to put every prospective candidate through such testing, nor is it practicable. Of course, how high or low candidates scored on these two attributes won't automatically ensure suitability on other job-related (as opposed to culture-related) criteria, so just attempting to select for attributes that provide a buffer against toxicity is quite problematic.

Some organisations actively select for competitiveness, autonomy, results focus, and power drive — the so-called masculine values (whether vested in a male or female). These individuals can be 'cloned' and form part of a dominant cultural force in an organisation: they become the adult equivalent of the so-called in-crowd, except they're much more likely to act like the Hollywood Brat Pack. I've seen it in parts of the banking sector, in the money market/stockbroking sector and in legal firms. The pressure is relentless, and work–life balance is nonexistent. There is little security as people are only as safe as their last deal, their annual billings, or their next transaction, but the goodies are there if you keep doing what's expected and admired (think the culture of the law firm in the novel and film *The Firm*). There is often an unspoken code and some weak sense of affiliation between the team members, as they provide immunity for each other from prosecution. That is not to say they are truly close. Such relationships are often shallow and opportunistic. The rate of burnout is high; the use of recreational drugs is endemic, and the incidence of depression is just beginning to be reported. So, ironically, some organisations want what good culture is *not* and actively select for it.

Existing Cultural Norms — The Cultural Context

Regardless of personality or personal style, some of us will find ourselves working in a system conducive to either the best or worst of behaviour. A close female friend and I laughed last week whilst talking about the power of unconscious patterns of behaviour. She explained how some weight had crept on with the birth of her children, and she had gone on a weight reduction program with considerable success a year before. She told me proudly how for months she had exerted real discipline, having declared to herself 'Sugar is the enemy!' However, the night before we got together, she explained she had gone to visit her aging mum. She walked up to the front door, kissed her mum, walked into the kitchen, went straight over to the pantry, and proceeded to devour almost half a packet of Tim Tams before she even registered that any of them were missing! Being back in her mum's house brought out her inner sugar fiend.

Similarly, I came across a senior manager while working in banking in my early career who had a terrible reputation for politicking and conniving. He was not well liked, and many staff volunteered that they didn't trust him. I met him at a Christmas party that year, and we talked about organisational politics. I shared my philosophy, which is to strive to find some genuine common ground with people and respect everyone. His look of disdain was something I will never forget as he told me how naïve I was. He said one had to be political to survive in an organisation.

Two years later, I heard from him. He reached out as a senior executive with another organisation. He wanted to bring me into his new company and had a project he wanted to discuss. He suggested we meet over lunch, and I was struck by how much younger and more relaxed he looked. He freely reminisced about his old job with our mutual employer. Unsolicited, he shared with absolute candour his belief that, when he looked back on how he had treated some people and some things he'd done, our previous organisation had 'brought out the worst' in him. He said he felt a lot of shame. He understood his ethical compass had gone awry as he jockeyed for power, recognition, and financial reward. Although we didn't specifically reference our conversation at the Christmas party, I sensed that it had been important for him to let me know he had turned his working life around. He has generously brought me in to three separate organisations over the course of the past fifteen years. From what I have observed, he is now a successful and respected executive.

The End Justifies the Means

Classical behavioural psychology would argue that we tend to repeat behaviours that provide a payoff. Conversely, behaviours are less likely to become extinct if they do not invoke negative consequences. Bad behaviour of any description will almost always gain a foothold because it achieves something for the perpetrator. But, of course, people in the organisation may decide to let the behaviour go unaddressed if the behaviour of the perpetrator provides benefit to them. In an article I wrote many years ago, I talked about a colleague who took up a position as general counsel to a prestigious law firm. Within a week, he came to me to ask for friendly advice. He had been told that a senior partner in the employee relations law practice was allegedly known to touch some of the young female staff and regularly said things considered highly inappropriate. From what my friend could gather, the only reason the partnership had tackled the issue was because the partner in question had now allegedly made an unwelcome overture to a client. That was when all hell broke loose. However, the offending partner brought in one million dollars worth of billings each year, and the firm had turned a blind eye to the intermittent rumblings from female staff, rationalising that his fine work in attracting business was keeping those women and others who worked there in a job.

My friend decided he couldn't live with the status quo and confronted the managing partner. With sweaty palms, he explained the cost to culture and iterated the reputational risk if someone were to make an external formal complaint. The managing partner agreed to tackle the issue, and the sexual harasser was packaged out. However, my friend said he thought it was a full six months before the partnership forgave him for creating such a problem for them. It is a classic case of shifting the blame and shooting the messenger.

Poor Self-Awareness and Low Self-Accountability

Ask most young children why they did something wrong, and they are likely to provide some extraneous reason as to why they resorted to something inappropriate. Likely retorts include 'I was hungry', 'She made me angry', or 'He kicked me first'. Grown-ups can make similar excuses.

Despite seemingly overwhelming evidence to the contrary, Lance Armstrong, disgraced Tour de France cyclist, insisted he had never been involved in doping. His most recent explanation for why former team mates gave evidence against him was 'they were jealous'.

I have been continually shocked and fascinated by the lengths some employees will go to defend the indefensible. Some have low self-awareness and typically take low self-responsibility. Some are willing to acknowledge they've erred but blame it on circumstance: 'Well, what are you meant to do when you've asked someone to do something three times and she keeps missing the deadline?' Whether we want to refer to this as low emotional intelligence, poor impulse control, or childishness, we see such behaviour in individuals that most certainly belies their chronological age.

Some of us are insecure and can't admit we are wrong. Ironically, that is probably an adaptive response, as I often observe such traits in those who've experienced the weight of extreme expectation or grown up in a strong blame culture. Some of us — often highly intelligent and prone to perfectionism — are so accustomed to being right or not being challenged that any suggestion we're at fault, or that the quality of work is not up to par, meets with indignation and even rage. This is one of the explanations why some high-achieving students don't cope well or become anxious when put in gifted programs. They find themselves competing with the best of the best, and they fear not measuring up. Without understanding their internal world, insensitive types will label them as emotionally unintelligent, soft, or noncoping, which only feeds the fear and self-loathing.

One of the biggest controversies to dog the Australian Rules Football code involved a former champion of the North Melbourne club, Wayne Carey. He had reportedly been such good friends with the team captain, Anthony Stevens, that everyone said they might as well have been brothers. Yet Carey rocked the football world when news broke that he was having an illicit relationship with Stevens's wife. Teammates were devastated. Stevens and his wife separated, and Carey, a decorated and revered premiership player, was cast out of the team. Even his coach, who loved him like a son, was gutted and walked away from him as what Carey did was so opposed to the culture of the club and its strong sense of kinship. Some time later, Sally Carey, the errant footballer's wife said in an interview that the problems resulted from the fact that no one — including herself, the coach, and her husband's agent — ever said 'no' to him. In other words, whatever he wanted, he got. His sense of invincibility and entitlement were extremely high, yet his sense of ethical accountability was seemingly very low.

Impoverished Skills/Modelling

Sadly, it is well established in the research literature that abusers tend to raise future abusers; that is, those who were subjected to domestic violence are far more likely to perpetrate domestic violence than the general population. Some of us are brought up with poor modelling around conflict resolution and assertion or how to use and abuse power to achieve outcomes. We may be taught how to intimidate as a means to an end. So some people are punitive or heavy-handed because it is a crude but effective tool to get what they want, regardless of the consequences for the other party. Of course, they may not believe that anything they've said or done could have had such an impact (low self-awareness). So there is no suggestion, as stated earlier, that there is an automatically malevolent intent: only a really clumsy or unsafe form of execution. However, if it works, or if there are no negative consequences, why will they necessarily stop?

Dealing With It Is Too Hard or Too Scary

Seeing the disincentive for individuals to moderate their bad behaviour is not the same as wondering why others around them allow it to happen. Some feel powerless or fearful to call offenders out on the behaviour. Some want to validate their own behaviour and may not see anything wrong with it. Some may even admire the tough negotiator as they see that person able to make things happen; in other words, the end justifies the means. In the case above of the lawyer partner who was sexually harassing staff, forget the hypocrisy, forget the intimidation, and forget the risk to brand. He was making big money for the firm and putting money into the pockets of the business owners — his fellow partners. Some would argue they were as morally bereft as he was.

So we may be able to understand that some people behave badly because it works (they get outcomes), because they don't know any better, because others may not hold up a mirror and make them accountable, or because it feels good and provides gratification. But why might it go unchecked, assuming people know about it?

I have painted a bleak picture of the bystander. The phenomenon of bystander apathy is a well-known and validated psychological construct. Sometimes the sheer number of people who witness something, diminishes their sense of personal responsibility; each waits for someone else to do the right thing. When that doesn't happen, they are seemingly validated for their own moral weakness or paralysis.

And, of course, some hold the belief that looking after others is not their responsibility. Not all of us feel accountable for preserving culture or protecting others. I've heard people acknowledge in honest moments that it reduces discomfort for them if someone else is getting attacked when they know it could otherwise be them. This may seem cowardly, but fear is an adaptive way to ensure the survival of the species. A study of Lucius Malfoy, his son Draco, and Draco's relationship with Crabb and Goyle in the *Harry Potter* series mimics this phenomenon.

Mental Illness and Personality Disorders

Many best-selling books and several wealthy speakers rose to prominence on the back of an exploration of sociopathy or psychopathy. An organisation of a few hundred or thousand people will undoubtedly have a couple or a few sociopaths, but not enough to explain the variance from the ethical compass and the prevalence of bad behaviour in some organisations and sectors. As we will discuss later, only 1 in 100 men and 1 in 200 women are sociopathic, defined in psychiatry as one variation of antisocial personality disorder. Therefore, some just don't care *or* feel that their sense of entitlement and desire or burning passion to get things done, excuses any means of getting there (Steve Jobs, founder of the Apple Corporation reportedly did this a lot). They are likely to become enraged or histrionic when challenged or cutting and vindictive so others become wary. They may also develop avoidance patterns, work around them, and if they become very pessimistic, leave.

Now we have discussed why damaging and disruptive behaviours can be established and maintained despite the potential costs. In the next chapter, you'll have a chance to assess your organisational health using the Warning Signs and Risk Factors Inventory and determine how protected you are from vulturesque behaviour and counterproductive workplace culture.

Chapter 4

Warning Signs and Risk Factors

ehaviours and cultural norms may be explained by a number of potential factors and context must be considered in determining what would or wouldn't be regarded as either normal or out of the ordinary. A staff member who is habitually unwilling to take leave may be engaging in fraudulent behaviour, may have conflict or stress at home, or may be extremely dedicated to his job!

Using the above example, it is clear that the presence of a warning sign or risk factor does not automatically dictate the existence of a vulture culture, particularly if the behaviour is not widespread. One warning sign or risk factor may not be enough. However it does make one more likely. Based on my experience, I have listed some of the most significant tell-tale warning signs (potential indicators) and risk factors (potential contributors or exacerbators) for the possible existence of vulture cultures. Several operating in combination may heighten the risk of wrongdoing and/or be more reliable indicators of a vulture culture.

How to Use the Inventory

Ask yourself:

In your workplace, what evidence do you see of the following in either individual employees, teams, branches or divisions that could:

- Seriously compromise the achievement of positive work outcomes or

- Indicate dysfunction, risk to health and safety or unlawful workplace behaviour?

If you consider a particular characteristic below is present or applies in your workplace, write down specific examples of the behaviour, consider the relative seriousness or risk of the warning sign and consider whether the characteristic is particular to a certain individual, department or pervasive across the organisation.

Corruption and Unethical Workplace Practice Warning Signs

- No policies or other instruments designed to outline or enforce acceptable standards of behaviour (e.g. company code of conduct or fraud policy)

- Inaccessible or infrequently publicised acceptable standards of behaviour (e.g. company code of conduct or fraud policy)

- Frequent noncompliance with company code of conduct such that aberrant behaviour becomes a norm (particularly with no apparent consequences)

- Poor or no pre-employment screening of candidates

- Poor or no screening and monitoring of vendors

- High proportion of enclosed offices so that privacy is maximised

- Portability of phone number extensions throughout the company (i.e. staff get to retain their phone number for extended periods)

- Staff required to take leave in short bursts only so are never away from work for very long
- Staff who insist on taking leave in short bursts only so are never away from work for very long
- Staff who won't relay phone calls to others when on leave
- Staff reluctant/refusing to take leave
- Major lifestyle change that might provoke high need (e.g. impending legal action, divorce or other acute financial pressure)
- Staff who are greedy or have over-extended themselves in terms of lifestyle
- Poorly-paid staff and/or those who work few hours per week (e.g. casual staff).
- Neurotic, suspicious or paranoid staff
- Overly cautious, vigilant staff
- Perceived psychopathy in staff
- Staff frequently at work after hours or on weekends
- Staff reluctant to provide access to their files or documents for others
- Staff working in (senior) accounting positions without appropriate checks and balances, adequate delegations policy and audit procedures
- Long term, over-friendly relationship with auditors
- Staff with known substance use or gambling addictions
- Tolerance of laxness in documenting transactions
- High tolerance of noncompliance with internal signoff procedures
- No hotline to report suspected fraud
- Tolerance of unethical behaviour
- Ready accessibility to desirable products, gifts, funds, entertainment and other benefits

- Evidence of (repeated) unethical decision-making in one or more staff
- Actual or perceived low risk of detection
- Actual or perceived low expectation of consequences
- Poor quality of organisation systems (both controls and detection)
- Poor or no review of password security
- Off work functions that are unsavoury, involve illegal activity including illicit drug use or fraternising with people of ill repute etc.
- Victimisation/ridicule or isolation of staff with high standard of personal ethics
- Minimal or absent ethics narrative (failure to maintain ethics dialogue with staff as a cultural norm)

Bullying or Harassment Warning Signs

- High absenteeism (even if authorised) particularly if a spike occurs
- Unauthorised absenteeism where staff fail to arrive for work and don't ring in
- Patterned absenteeism (e.g. Monday's, Friday's or days when particular people are in)
- Other forms of time theft including clock watching, (unreasonable) private use of social media, web browsing and internet gaming
- Unacceptable or unusual number of requests for transfer
- Unacceptable or unusual levels of turnover (particularly in a depressed economy)
- Turnover in discrete staff groups after a very short period (particularly senior roles or specialists)
- Exit interviews pointing to the existence of toxic workplace

culture (particularly where 'testimony' is strongly aligned with other views expressed).

- Alleged wrongdoings reported via anonymous complaints in writing, employee or whistleblower hotline, or employee opinion survey
- Grievance activity citing leadership, bullying or unsafe behaviour as the antecedent event/s
- Inappropriate or abusive content or tone in log book entries left for staff on other shifts
- Inappropriate or abusive content or tone in email correspondence
- Staff being 'flamed' on noticeboards, at meetings, on work websites (e.g. intranet) or non-work social media sites (e.g. Facebook or Twitter)
- Excessive or over reliance on email as form of communication (as an avoidance strategy)
- Email or memo 'slanging matches' that go unchecked
- Politicising of emails where others are cc'ed or blind cc'ed to work correspondence to defend/justify action or inaction (i.e. motivated by fear)
- Politicising of emails where others are cc'ed or blind cc'ed to work correspondence to 'flame', blame or put staff under pressure (motivated by control or desire for retaliation)
- Complaints about stress
- High incidence of accidents and near misses
- Evidence of avoidance patterns with staff minimising contact with others with whom they are required to work
- Staff routinely congregating in tea rooms or smoking areas to avoid work or difficult personalities
- Black humour or derogatory banter about minority groups by staff or managers (particularly if it goes unchecked)

- Staff engaging in indirect communication about unacceptable behaviour with work colleagues/friends but not able to confront perpetrators
- Claims or evidence that staff have given feedback to perpetrators that has not resulted in behaviour change
- Reluctance for staff to attend meetings (particularly if certain people are in attendance)
- Fear or tension in meetings that result in lack of contribution, withdrawal
- Aggressive and abusive behaviour in meetings
- Aggressive or abusive behaviour in meetings that is not 'called'
- Office banter changing for the worse; stories told that don't reflect resilience or optimism
- Staff voicing cynicism or mistrust about willingness of the company/a manager to do something about 'bad' behaviour
- External formal complaints or legal action against the company or individual employees
- Staff or managers trivialising bad behaviour possibly evidenced by jokes and innuendo
- Staff or managers discouraging recipients of bad behaviour to escalate issues to management
- Obvious signs of personality change, withdrawal, depression, stress in staff members
- Recent arrival of minority group members to the organisation with low tolerance for difference
- Under-resourced teams with excessive pressure to deliver
- High velocity change agenda (includes well-conceived change that may create insecurity or pressure in some staff)
- Lack of demonstrated care when excessive demands are placed on staff

- High levels of occupational stress (e.g. police, air traffic controllers) that add to unacceptable levels of workplace stress
- (Threat of) performance management used without justification to harass or intimidate staff
- Legitimate performance management administered in such a way as to cause intimidation or humiliation for staff
- Decline in morale, engagement, laughter, willingness to socialise outside work hours
- Low incidence of volunteerism for new projects or staff committees
- 'Presenteeism' — staff who stay when they really want to go
- Overzealous leadership that is overly task focussed with insufficient emphasis on people management and support
- Readying the organisation for takeover or buyout (pressure for productivity or profitability)
- Laissez faire management style or absent management (e.g. virtual team, dispersed team)
- Excessive guilt articulated or demonstrated by staff who failed to act on poor behaviour
- Admission of wrongdoing by staff in the absence of formal complaints
- Victimisation of complainant/s
- Victimisation of alleged respondent/s
- Victimisation of suspected witnesses to investigations
- Victimisation, ridicule or isolation of staff with high work ethic or commitment to quality
- Victimisation, ridicule or isolation of staff with high commitment to their organisation
- Minority groups in the workplace
- Poor or no EEO ethics and OH&S narrative (failure to maintain fair treatment dialogue with staff as a cultural norm)

- Poor or no investment in leadership development to cultivate bench strength in supportive leadership
- Poor change leadership capability

Discrimination Warning Signs

- Staff complaints about nepotism
- Staff complaints about favouritism
- Well qualified internal staff who desist from applying for advertised positions
- Low trust/cynicism about selection procedures
- Widespread bitterness or surprise at candidate appointments (beyond those who applied and were unsuccessful)
- Individuals promoted (i.e. slotted in) to positions in breach of company recruitment policy
- Accurate staff predictions by staff about the identity of successful candidates when vacancies arise? (excluding standout applicants based on merit)
- Absence of panel interviews as standard
- No publication of transparent role-related selection criteria
- Selection criteria publicised but seemingly not applied
- Discomfort/reluctance to provide feedback to 'unsuccessfuls'
- Perpetuation of homogenous work groups such that minority groups or those with protected attributes continue to miss out beyond what would be feasible in context
- Lack of progression of candidates with protected attributes (e.g. disabled where reasonable accommodations may be required to be made by the company if the candidate was successful)
- Differential pay and conditions for work of equal value based on nepotism, favouritism or a protected attribute (e.g. age, gender etc.)
- Minority groups in the workplace

- Minority groups in the workplace where no or poor cultural education has been provided
- A history of victimisation of those who are 'different'

Note: Many of the warning sings listed under Bullying and Harassment may apply to environments where discrimination is occurring (e.g., high absenteeism, high turnover, complainant victimisation etc.)

Incompetent Leadership Warning Signs

- Laissez Faire or absent management of teams that require an active manager presence
- Ineffectual/weak management (failure to do the 'hard stuff')
- Autocratic management style
- Conflict-averse management style
- Suffocating management style; over-controlling (particularly when staff are highly competent)
- Enmeshed or friendship-based management
- Mistrust of worker competence
- Under-developed coaching culture
- Poor or no effort in induction of new or inexperienced staff
- Unauthorised absenteeism where staff fail to arrive for work and don't ring in
- Patterned absenteeism (e.g. Monday's, Friday's that goes undetected and or is not addressed)
- Other forms of time theft including clock watching, (unreasonable) private use of social media, web browsing and internet gaming
- Poor (unarrested) productivity
- Poor (unarrested) work quality
- Low personal motivation with poor matching of aspirations and skills with tasks and roles

- Email or memo 'slanging matches' that go unchecked
- Politicising of emails where others are cc'ed or blind cc'ed unnecessarily to work correspondence to 'flame', blame or put staff under pressure
- Unacceptable or unusual levels of turnover (particularly in a depressed economy)
- Turnover in staff after a very short period (particularly senior roles or specialists)
- Punitive or retaliatory management when staff make mistakes
- Punitive or retaliatory management when staff show initiative that is not supported
- Management that takes undue credit for staff contributions
- Management that tolerates chronic underperformance or misconduct because of personal relationship with staff member
- Management that tolerates misconduct (e.g. sexual harassment or bullying) because staff member is a high performer (e.g. top salesperson)
- Failure to institute any change program on a large scale high impact change
- Poor execution of a change program resulting in unnecessary strees
- Victimisation, ridicule or isolation of staff with high work ethic or commitment to quality
- Victimisation, ridicule or isolation of staff with high commitment to their organisation
- Off work functions that are unsavoury or involve illegal activity or potentially bring the organisation into disrepute e.g. sports gambling, attending strip clubs etc.

PART TWO

'Various Species of Vulture '

Chapter 5

Corruption and Unethical Business Practices

*'The more you see, the more you play, the more
the horror fades away'.*

— *Call of Duty* computer gamer

One manifestation of destructive workplace behaviours is to engage in practices that could destroy the company. Corrupt, even criminal behaviour and unethical work practices can only exist in a culture that allows, condones, and incentivises them.

The way in which we discuss business ethics here does not automatically imply illegal activity. However, true to our broad definition of a vulture culture that preys on everything that's good and wholesome in a company, unethical business practices, particularly those that occur for personal gain and with high reputational and other associated risks, definitely match the description.

Morality As a Subjective Construct

Defining and exploring corrupt behaviour is vexed. Corruption, just like morality, is a relative concept. People have a moral code they live by: the so-called 'moral compass'. That is not to say everyone's moral compass points in the same direction. People don't always agree with each other on the biggest moral imperatives.

For example a government may argue that the introduction of a new tax on carbon emissions from relevant businesses is a major step toward reducing global warming and that it would be immoral for us *not* to take the long-term view to protect the future for generations to come. The opposition might argue that such a policy is fundamentally immoral as it would threaten the livelihood of thousands of workers from those manufacturing and mining businesses affected by the tax.

Another example comes from our prison system. While one might argue that armed robbers and murderers are entirely corrupt individuals with no moral compass, it is well validated that many of those offenders have their own distinctive moral code in respect of their hatred for paedophiles and murderers of children. They are known to have acted on that belief while incarcerated with a great deal of protection afforded by other inmates. Anyone who aggresses against a paedophile in a prison is unlikely to be found out.

It is mostly due to the subjectivity and individuality of a person's moral compass that business has sought to eliminate the margin of error through explicit rules: guidelines coupled with those aspects of governance enshrined in law. At the end of the day, businesses are obligated to inform employees of codes of conduct, legislative requirements, internal audit requirements, and the like, but it is then incumbent upon employees in their decision-making to get it right every time.

Corruption and Unethical Business Practices

Corruption is an evocative term that varies in meaning. We could refer to corruption in the sense of accepting illegal bribes, for example, police accepting payment from underworld factions to miscarry justice by 'losing' evidence. Or, in a behavioural sense, corruption could connote leading someone else astray. Both definitions are apt in the context of the vulture culture, and we address both in this chapter.

Every national culture has its own mores around what it considers acceptable and outside the accepted norm. And we can all understand the challenges for multinationals trading in many countries where the rules vastly differ from those of their sovereign country. Bribes may be regarded as entirely unethical in some countries but may be routine protocols of business in other countries. One person's 'kickback' may be regarded by someone else as no more than a strategic facilitation payment that gets the job done.

The World Bank attempts an operational definition of corruption by asking four questions of people needing to decide what's right or wrong.

- Transparency — Am I happy to talk about it or for others to know about it?
- Accountability — Do I report my actions to someone else? Do they hold me to standards?
- Reciprocity — Would I feel hurt or aggrieved if others did the same thing?
- Generalisation — Would it harm society if everyone did the same thing?

If we extrapolate from this simple but sound definition, then we have some way of construing unethical business practices. The practices may involve doing things under the table rather than on the table. Offending employees may be a law unto themselves. They would not necessarily expect or tolerate other members of staff doing what they do without sanction, and the pain for others inside and outside the organisation could be immense.

Simply put, unethical business practices may or may not be unlawful, but they could place the organisation at significant risk commercially, reputationally, and culturally.

We are currently living in the very long tail of a debilitating global financial crisis. Endless stories abound about the people, organisations, and their fatal misguided assumptions and decisions that served as a catalyst for such major economic and societal impacts.

We get the culture we deserve; we get the behaviour we are prepared to tolerate. By tolerate I also mean enable, condone, incentivise, rationalise, defend, deny, or unwittingly excuse through inaction. Counterproductive workplace behaviours (those volitional or voluntary behaviours contrary to the public and/or company good) can occur in the context of corrupt and unethical leadership or absent, weak, or incompetent leadership. When we read in the paper about a scandal and senior executives who claim they had no idea what was going on, they may not necessarily be lying, but that doesn't necessarily excuse them. The media and social commentators will swiftly remind them it happened on their watch.

The causes and contributing factors to counterproductive workplace behaviours fall under two basic headings: greed/corruption (i.e., immorality) and incompetence or poor decision making. The forms of counterproductive workplace behaviours researched the most thoroughly are time theft (i.e., withdrawal of labour in all its manifestations) and antisocial behaviour (e.g., theft, workplace violence, or sexual harassment).

Withdrawal of Labour (Not Being There or Being There Without Being There)
Protest

Withdrawal of labour can include volitional absence, lateness, 'presenteeism'[1] (being physically present but disengaged or inef-

---

1 More recently, the word 'presenteeism' has acquired an alternative meaning in the organisational literature. The word has also come to denote the phenomenon whereby people who are unwell choose to come to work rather than stay home due to any of several positive or negative motivators (e.g., high commitment or engagement, concerns about using up sick leave, or other negative consequences of not being there, such as being seen as uncommitted or anxiety about others replacing them in an insecure environment). This can be regarded as an organisational issue that goes beyond personal choice because of the potential for cross-infection and resulting mass absence. Interestingly, I have witnessed an increase in 'resenteeism' about this form of presenteeism, as other staff may view the decision of unwell staff to attend for work as selfish and costly. This is one reason some organisations spend large dollars on flu vaccinations for staff each winter.

fectual) and turnover. My position is that in certain cases this is immoral because the person is being paid to work and isn't there. I draw a sharp distinction between those who volitionally make themselves absent (on the premises or at home because they are either lazy or protesting) versus those who exercise the legitimate right to take time out because they are unwell or not coping.

Another important qualification in this discussion is that some organisations make unreasonable demands on people or lead so poorly such that they erode engagement, and employees are more likely to seek to absent themselves from short staffing, onerous obligations, or punitive inhospitable culture. Indeed, some of my clients actively encourage staff to take off recovery days when they deem themselves to be struggling. Typically, this occurs where staff are in frontline customer service delivery roles and frayed tempers or burnout can lead to destructive conflict and/or inferior service. What is under discussion here is withdrawal of labour as a means of protest without an automatic presumption that the reasons (or the need) for doing so are immoral or invalid.

It is both ironic and disturbing that an employee can choose not to come to work and or turn up and get paid and still choose 'not to come to work'. Consulting to a state government department some years ago, I had an employee give a wry smile and point to a desk and an empty chair. He said: 'See that desk. Mac built his new house from that chair. We all knew about it, including every time he and his missus had a fight with the builder. If not for the fact we were so hopping mad he wasn't working, we could have made lots of suggestions about the layout and energy saving strategies'. When I asked whether this behaviour was 'called', my erstwhile employee said the closest they came was the occasional sarcastic remark, which Mac either 'didn't get or conveniently ignored'. Any serious suggestion Mac should have been managed was met with derision because there was such pessimism about management's willingness and ability to do anything about it. 'How could we prove it?' was the weak excuse a middle manager gave when an exasperated colleague finally demanded that something be done. The colleague suggested the manager swap roles with him for a couple of weeks and then he'd no doubt be asked to give input into the colour of the floor tiles in the upstairs bathroom!

Absence

Simply put, absence is not showing up for work. Employees may be no-shows, flout requirements to notify their employer within a specified period, and therefore effectively abandon their employment. Given the probability that organisations can and do act on such flagrant disrespect/disregard for explicit policy and procedures, it is more likely that staff will make contact and invoke other mechanisms in their attempts to legitimate authorised leave.

They may use sick leave without being sick, use carer's leave illegitimately, mount grievances, take unlawful industrial action, lodge work insurance claims and cite fabricated unsafe work practices or other occupational health and safety (OHS) concerns as to why they cannot show up for work.

For example, at some construction firms and government building regulators with which I've consulted, the staff would remark bemusedly about the debilitating effects of safety-inspired industrial action just prior to a concrete pour. I remember saying I didn't think it got any worse than that. I was immediately corrected by a manager who said the only thing worse than an OHS representative/union delegate turning mischievous just prior to a concrete pour was the one who became so in the middle of one!

Similarly, when working a number of years ago with an international airline with an Australian presence, I was struck by the widespread industrial action regarding fumes that were supposedly permeating the cabin and causing cabin staff to feel unwell. Some would refuse to fly certain sectors. What was fascinating was that the airline did eventually discover (and admit) there had been some nonhazardous emissions on a particular model that could cause nausea and dizziness for some sensitive passengers and crew. However, for months after this situation was identified and corrected (those planes were initially grounded and subsequent repairs made), some staff, and typically those known to be disengaged or aggrieved, continued to insist there were problems with other planes in the fleet and protested loudly and publicly. Not surprisingly, these concerns were investigated and found to be without merit, but the allegations and the 'symptoms' persisted for some months. The behaviour ceased only when the airline drew a line in the sand and announced it would take decisive disciplinary action against anyone who refused to report for shifts citing those safety concerns on planes where no hazards were known to exist. Miraculously, all staff recovered overnight.

In both the concrete pour and the airline fleet nausea examples, withdrawal of labour was seemingly used as a form of protest. There was more reason for people to opt out than to want to do the job they were being paid to do. Something was wrong at the organisation!

Taking a day off work illegitimately and claiming it as a personal paid leave day in Australia is such a recognised phenomenon that we have a colloquial term for it — 'chucking a sickie'. Yet I know many staff and managers in organisations who have not taken sick leave and consequently built up so many days owed that it begins to be unsustainable for the business. This may be borne of admirable dedication, proneness to addictive behaviour, delusions of indispensability, or fear of missing out. Some organisations have acted on this unacceptable bank of leave by creating a policy decreeing that staff sick leave cannot go past a certain amount as it creates an unsustainable burden on the organisation in the form of a financial vulnerability on the balance sheet if they were to pay out sick leave. Some of us are working very hard — even too hard — and others not hard enough. Both phenomena speak to problematic culture.

Choosing not to come to work when one is paid to do so says something. It may say something about the toxicity of the workplace, including under-resourcing and the sense of futility in trying to do so much with so little. It may be catalysed by the manager who refuses to acknowledge and appreciate good work such that people start to develop a growing resentment. It can reflect a chaotic environment, particularly in the context of ill-conceived or poorly sold change, such that the only way for the staff to exert control over an out-of-control existence is to choose not to come to work. It can become a form of self-medication for those who spend so many days metaphorically 'swimming in a rip' that they need a rest and recovery day just as the Tour de France cyclists do over the three weeks of the race. In a healthier environment, one in which people can be emotionally honest with each other, there is more freedom for people to put their hands up and admit they are doing it tough or need time out. In less healthy or safe cultures, the same need goes underground.

'Presenteeism'

Some people have said they find it hard to imagine colleagues can seemingly get away with doing so little in a climate that's tough and pessimistic and where teams have been stripped back and run lean. Here, as always, there are some important qualifications. Some people are masters at looking busy. Others don't even attempt to look busy. Still others are busy doing the work of the organisation to a high standard, some to a low standard despite their best attempts, and still others are genuinely busy doing a whole lot of stuff they're not paid to do or that doesn't provide an adequate return on the organisation's investment.

Most of us love the person who runs the footy tipping each year. However, if the same person runs the footy tipping, heads up the social club, is the OHS delegate, and is regularly out of the office attending union-sponsored training, then we might ask when does she do her day job?

Every reader of this book probably knows someone who puts up their hand for so many portfolios. A colleague and I dub them the 'milliners' because they are always sporting so many hats! Of course, this is patently unfair if all of these morale-boosting and health-enhancing activities are their day job and their official title is Director of Inspiration, Engagement, and Collective well-being. What if someone is anointed to all these roles because she has the trust and affection of the people and possesses excellent interpersonal skills? Fair enough. Then let's give that person that role legitimately and take into account the amount of time this person devotes to it so we do not put an undue burden on her colleagues.

I differentiate between the legitimate role transparently understood by all and the one designed by the jobholder to take into account all her own loves and preferences without consultation and with burdensome consequences for others. Again, the leaders are at fault if they let this go on and refuse to do anything about it. We can find an inherent immorality in vastly disproportionate workloads and favouritism where some staff get the freedom to craft the job of their dreams and others inherit the rest of the work, which becomes their personal nightmare. The weak or absent leader allows this to happen, and how much worse for the staff if it's the leader who's done the interior design on her own job and is not minding the store.

As an example, let's look at Joe Gregory. He was one of the original so-called 'Ponderosa Boys', President and Chief Operating Officer of Lehman Brothers from 2002 to 2008. Author Vicky Ward wrote in her book, *The Devil's Casino*, of 'the foibles of men, the corrosive influence of money, and the dangers of hubris'. She suggests in her book that Gregory stopped minding the store, that he had never professed to be a trader as much as a banker but found a portfolio in his later years with the firm that consumed him. Gregory decided that the ultimate in competitive advantage for Lehman Brothers was to be diversity and inclusion. In this respect, he showed admirable foresight. He was conscious of the outrageous gender imbalance at the top of the 7,000-strong organisation and saw it as a huge coup when Erin Callan became the new CFO in 2008. He became the public champion of the firm's Gay, Lesbian, Bisexual and Transgender network and was a staunch advocate for its Women in Leadership enterprise. However, it is widely acknowledged that he stopped looking at and asking about the numbers, arguably with disastrous consequences.

We will come back to the extraordinary phenomenon that was Lehman Brothers in a separate discussion of lax and incompetent leadership. Indeed, it's not a crime to be mediocre or just competent. Not everyone can be as efficient and disciplined as everyone else. It is also not a crime — in fact, it is reasonable and appropriate — for people to derive joy, nourishment, and possibly even friendship whilst at work. But this cannot come at the expense of the job to be done. Presenteeism, as opposed to the enthusiastic communication and off-subject banter of people who enjoy working shoulder to shoulder, implies something volitional about enjoying take-home pay whilst opting out.

Time Theft — Technology

The introduction of certain technologies to the workplace has been a double-edged sword. Many cannot imagine their working day without the use of brilliant, time-saving tools like the smartphone and iPad. However, I also await the sad inevitability of a Diagnostic and Statistical Manual of the American Psychiatric Association that officially recognises technology addictions (seen in popular phrases such as the so-called 'crackberry culture' and in frenzied Facebook checking, perpetual phone holding, or texting compulsion). The visible signs of compulsive behaviour, high anxiety, increasing tolerance or dependence over time, and withdrawal (when forced to turn off phones) are telltale signs of addiction.

Admittedly, some of these tools are designed to enhance productivity and make information and communication accessible anytime and anywhere. While that might well apply in the case of e-mail, the same cannot be said of a round of internet Scrabble at the work desk, a few surreptitious games of Angry Birds during a meeting, or an extended period on the Expedia website planning one's next holiday. Strictly speaking, it is not within this book's scope to wax lyrical about the psychosocial impacts of such tools when people are unable or unwilling to establish some semblance of balance in their use except where the misuse or abuse of such tools says something insidious about the culture or in turn influences culture negatively. But one thing seems certain: rife abuse of such tools constituting time theft is very likely to indicate poor workplace engagement.

Why might this be occurring? It may be driven by employees who are testing the bounds of reasonableness and go unchecked by ineffectual leaders or leaders who themselves offend. Or, such unchecked activity may indicate dysfunction within the organisation such that individuals are not motivated to regulate nonwork distractions. Either way, the vultures are circling and the culture is probably in trouble.

Decisions regarding whether to permit employees to access the Internet and social media for work have given organisations serious headaches. Virtually all large organisations I have observed attempt to bar access to some websites on the basis that employees have no business need to access them (e.g., eBay) or that they pose unacceptable risk (e.g., pornography sites). Others have said they 'trust' their people to decide when and where they access websites. If they are trusted to do Internet banking at lunchtime, and the tools of the trade enable this, then why not trust them to restrict the use of social media to authorised breaks too? Of course, this is fine where people demonstrate they are worthy of that trust and are able to make sound decisions about how they manifest the faith the employer puts in them. If their view of what's reasonable collides with that of others in the workplace, are there the same cultural checks and balances as required for other indiscretions or acts of noncompliance?

Spending time in work hours visiting social media sites, discussing home revisions, or starting gossip at the water cooler reflects something of the character of the individuals who commit it, the context that provokes it, and the culture that allows it to go without cessation and without consequences.

A few years ago, I ran a workshop on sexual harassment that included a piece on the appropriateness of access to e-mail and the Internet. The ban on Internet use hit a nerve with one participant. He argued his firm had no right to give him a tool of the trade that allowed him to stay in over lunch to do Internet banking, access an online grocery store to shop, allow him to make enquiries about an upcoming concert without getting caught up in a queue at the entertainment box office, and then become so indignant when someone attempted to access an Internet site the company found offensive. He argued that if the organisation gave employees a tool that suited its purposes and enabled it to get its pound of flesh, what right did the organisation have to dictate how that tool of trade could and couldn't be used? He and others were indignant that several staff at a major telecommunications company had been summarily dismissed because they accessed pornographic websites.

I suggested we find our answer in a parallel example. An astute participant piped up and said that if we accepted the premise that staff should have unfettered access to tools their employer pro-vided and were allowed to self-regulate (or not), then it followed that employees at a butcher shop could decide to use any knives they were provided ... on each other! Having worked with a gourmet meat company that supplied the high end of the hospitality industry, I shared the details of its explicit ground rules, which were that if staff so much as raised their voices at each other when working in close proximity with such 'weapons', they were in danger of being dismissed. I recalled the managing director of this highly successful family business saying that this simple rule had served his business well. He had acted on the rule twice in twenty-five years and didn't regret taking decisive action when weighing it against the alternative, which was a dangerously permissive environment. There was no doubt his people knew where they stood on workplace conflict and aggression if they wanted to keep their jobs.

Opportunism and Theft

The counterproductive workplace behaviours discussed above are examples of production-based deviances (time theft, absenteeism, presenteeism, etc). Some violations in organisations — those typically associated with corruption and unlawful behaviour — are, in fact, property-based. It is well established that the propensity for people to engage in corrupt behaviour, including theft and vandalism, for example, hinges on a few intersecting elements. Such unlawful practices cost organisations annually in the billions of dollars and are on the rise in Australia. [2]

Common reasons why employees steal are:

- Their morale or engagement is low, so their ethical attachment to the company is weak.

---

2 Incidence of employee theft international foundation of protection officers IFPO estimates employee dishonesty (lost and stolen) is over $50 billion annually. 75% of employees steal (steal, use or misuse without permission) at least once and at least half the 75% steal multiple times. Reasons for stealing include low morale, embittered employee, perceived underpaid or under-appreciated, minimal consequences, lack of control over inventory so no preventive measures (i.e. opportunity (as the leading cause of theft), low likelihood if detection, bystander apathy or fear of victimisation).

- They see largesse, extravagance or ostentatiousness in owners or executives who 'don't deserve it' and think the company has so much it 'won't miss anything'.

- They feel wronged or embittered, which justifies some form of punishment or retribution.

- They feel underpaid or underappreciated for the significant contribution they make and justify some form of payback or compensation.

- They have an acute need, such as a gambling addiction, drug addiction, or high personal debt.

- They have the opportunity. Opportunity is the leading cause of theft. If preventive and detection measures are weak, and the risk of detection is low, employees experience low anxiety about being caught.

- The consequences for transgressions are minimal. The company may not have processes in place or fail to enforce them, so employees have low anxiety about being punished.

- The behaviours may be normed as acceptable at work either because other staff engage in them or don't call them, so employees become inoculated against any internal perception of wrongdoing.

- Employees lack integrity. This is why selecting people of 'sound character' (we will return to this) is a commonsensical imperative.

When it's all said and done, tight processes, monitoring, and enforcement are critical but only half the answer as they restrict opportunity and may increase perception about the likelihood of being caught. The flip side of that is working on engagement by modelling good behaviour, treating people well, developing them, and having them predict negative (even very serious) consequences for messing up because they know such counterproductive behaviours are culturally aberrant. We need to close down loopholes and ease of access but also treat staff well, pay them fairly, motivate and engage them. Instilling company pride and attachment is one form of defence, especially as bystander apathy theory dictates that other staff cannot necessarily be counted on to report a wrongdoing. 'I don't want to get involved' can be a common mantra in less accountable cultures.

Another important factor is choosing people who like what the company stands for, so the selection decision is important. I talk about the importance of something as old-fashioned as good character in chapter 10 on Organisational Strategies.

How Corruption and Unethical Business Practice Conspire to Create Vulture Cultures

In the most fundamental of ways, corruption and unethical business practices set the tone for organisational life. Even where sole individuals are perpetrating deeds that are unethical, unlawful, or otherwise toxic, much of their remaining energy goes into concealment. If we contemplate the empirical research that says such behaviour occurs in environments where a small risk of detection meets a high tolerance of such behavioural norms, the potential for organisational damage is very real (source).

In an era where whole teams of investigative reporters doggedly research companies and governments to fill the front pages of newspapers, in which a company reputation is simply a mouse click away from viral exposure, where one disgruntled employee can announce his boredom in fewer than 140 characters on Twitter and flame his boss on Facebook as he exits the business, we see the critical importance of developing quality processes, a high compliance culture, and a strong moral tone as well as working to engage staff who want to see the business flourish.

Corruption and other forms of unethical work practice can only exist in a culture that allows, condones, incentivises, defends, ignores, protects, and excuses them.

Chapter 6

Workplace Bullying

Don't even think to ask people to contribute,
much less innovate, if you can't meet their basic needs
for safety and security.

In the twenty-five years I have worked in corporate and industry, I have seen the deviant and the dastardly as well as the misguided and the malcontent (who take their unhappiness out on others). Therefore, I have seen the unwitting bully and the highly intentional malicious bully who gets off on doing someone else's head in, actively and deliberately contributing to an unsafe workplace and the destruction of the subject's self-confidence.[1]

A serious exploration of the phenomenon of workplace bullying is not possible without understanding the philosophical construct of the difference between intent and impact.

---

1 The word 'victim' connotes helplessness, and I would prefer not to imply or perpetuate the notion that targets or subjects of bullying have no recourse. Indeed, some people are the subjects of incessant and pervasive bullying with seemingly no ill effects, although some experience serious deleterious effects of bullying. Further, bullying is likely to be unsolicited and unwelcome, inherently infringes on the rights of the other party, and is almost always unhelpful.

Many of the assumptions below go to the issue of intent versus impact. As a rule of thumb, common law in Australia does not presume intent in relation to an act; it is the impact that counts. We are effectively judged by our actions, not our motives. What is easier to assess? I would say behaviour over thoughts. Herein lies a paradox. Not only might one not intend to bully but do so anyway, but others around the person can condone the unacceptable behaviour because the 'end justifies the means'. Some people who inappropriately wield power can appear in the vulture culture to create some positive impacts. They get stuff done. I am reminded of a quote from the popular TV series, *NCIS* where the lead character Gibbs says of the Field Agent Tony Di Nozzo: 'You may not like his methods, but you gotta love the results'.

Exploding Myths

Firstly, some myths that need to be exploded:

- **Bullies are sadists who know what they're doing.** Many writers have declared bullying is all about power. That may be true, but not every bully bullies intentionally. Having said that, unintentional bullying can also create significant damage and lead to a pronounced lack of safety for the subject of the attention.

- **Bullies are insecure people who bully to make themselves feel big.** This can be true, but not always. Some bully because they like the power it gives them, while others bully because that is all they know based on what they have seen. If you think of the Draco Malfoy character in the Harry Potter series, we understand Draco better when we meet his parents. At first, his father is happy to be seen in that dark company and has a certain stature and status as a member of Voldemort's inner circle. However, as we progress through the series, we see Voldemort's blood lust increase such that even Lucius Malfoy becomes terrified of Voldemort. Having originally pandered to the powerful leader in a sycophantic way, he does so later out of pure terror, knowing Voldemort could kill him, his wife, or Draco on a whim. In this situation, Lucius is adopting the norms of a tyrannical regime out of love for his family and his fear of death, not because of any lack of self-confidence.

- **One rotten act constitutes bullying.** Bullying is defined under most Australian OH&S law as repeated unreasonable behaviour that creates a risk to health and safety. Thus one act of bully-esque behaviour may not pass the threshold for bullying, but this doesn't make it okay or 'ignorable'. Bullying under most legislation must be repeated or constitute a pattern of behaviour. That is not to say that a one-off incident of abusive, aggressive, or undermining behaviour can't be hugely distressing for someone based on the context, the personalities of the two parties, and the way in which the behaviour is construed. I address such one-off occurrences with clients and perpetrators as examples of 'inappropriate workplace behaviour' and potential misconduct, which may still evoke the same disciplinary process but without the use of the bullying label. The word 'bullying' has in fact permeated our modern lexicon to alarming proportions. The child in the schoolyard who makes a nasty, thoughtless comment to another might be labelled a bully. Yet just because a nicer or more emotionally intelligent child may not use such language, doesn't automatically make the first child a bully.

- **Bullying is relentless perpetration of the same act over and over again.** Bullying, even if presenting as a pattern of behaviour, does not have to involve the same behaviour over and over again. It could be a number of differing incidents or events that, when put together, contribute to a person feeling unsafe.

- **Bullying is typically verbal or physical abuse on racial, religious, or gender grounds.** Bullying does not have to go to a protected attribute or what is called under equal opportunity law a 'prohibited ground of discrimination'. Bullying may include verbal abuse or psychological harassment, but it does not have to be racially motivated or include gender-based taunts or ridicule. It is the unsafety as a consequence (regardless of whether intended) that makes it bullying, not because it is racist, sexist, or ageist in substance.

- **Exclusion or isolation could not possibly be bullying.** Some bullies have tried to tell me at an investigation interview they could not possibly have bullied, as they haven't *spoken* with the alleged victim in months. In other forms of harassment or discrimination, the perpetrator must engage in some way with the victim. In bullying, the damage may be caused by actively excluding or isolating the victim or utilising nonverbal gestures or expressions to intimidate a subject.

- **Why should we have to be friends with everyone?** Bullying legislation does not mandate friendship in the workplace. People are not being asked to include all staff in all work-related and non-work-related activity. It is the pattern of offensive behaviour that in the eyes of a reasonable person could constitute a risk to health and safety (either psychological or physical) that makes behaviour bully-esque.

- **It's the victims' fault *because* they are weak and just ask to be pushed around.** It is offensive and untrue to say that bullying happens only to weak people who become easy targets for bullies. Whether motivated by boredom, sadistic tendencies, or jealousy, anyone can bully and be bullied. Some cowardly bullies will prey on those who are less assertive, have few if any home supports or allies at work, and show they are clearly adversely affected by the attention they are getting, which makes the bully feel powerful and feeds his or her ego. That bully is often insecure and needs to assert himself or herself and feel powerful in ways we would consider socially inappropriate. However, some people are targeted because in fact they are popular, attractive, intelligent, or even happy or positive. They just have to be different in some way. Nobel Prize laureate Dr. Barry Marshall from Fremantle, Western Australia reportedly was maligned and ridiculed for years by the posh English Harley Street medical establishment when he discovered that almost all ulcers were caused by a bacterium, *Helicobacter pylori*, and not by stress. He was eventually compelled by his frustration with his colleagues to dramatically demonstrate the logic of his findings by drinking a concoction of the bacterium and giving himself gastritis, which he was subsequently able to cure!

- **I wouldn't have to resort to bullying if people would only do their job.** This already sounds like an excuse or justification for heavy-handed treatment even though the sad fact might be that some staff don't pull their weight until someone threatens them with negative consequences. In a workplace, particularly a large one, there will be all types of people on the payroll, from those with a naturally high work ethic to those who come to work to look busy doing nothing much in particular. We will usually see close to a normal distribution with the majority willing to do a reasonable day's work for a reasonable day's pay if they get halfway good leadership, consistency, and rewards for outcomes (if not effort). However, a system needs a homeostatic mechanism to keep it in balance. The more autocratic and punitive the leader, the less likely the staff are to raise their heads above the parapet for fear of having them shot off.

- **There's nothing wrong with a 'robust' environment if everyone's okay with it.** In some systems, everyone treats everyone else badly. This 'normed' behaviour sometimes passes for black humour or 'knocking' humour, which is a particular feature of Australian humour — having a laugh at someone else's expense. However, it could be argued that if everyone is okay with it, it's not likely to be bullying, and is it humour or something else? A new person could come into a workplace and react differently to those who have decided that what they do is okay, or new people can come into the system and decide that the behaviour must be okay or desirable and then proceed to step over the invisible line from acceptable into unacceptable because that's what others are doing.

- **People bully very deliberately to get what they want (because it often works).** This can most certainly be true. However, I have heard this stated mostly by people who think that someone *always* premeditates bullying as a tactical methodology to beat others into figurative submission (i.e., agreement or compliance). Some of the respondents I have worked with in bullying complaints are genuinely shocked and dismayed that not only has someone else construed their behaviour as bullying but also that the complainants believed the respondents set out to intimidate or abuse them from the get-go. The fact is people who bully may have a profound lack of awareness of the impact of their actions. In other words, they may exhibit really clumsy communication skills and regress into punitive or vicious behaviour when they don't get their way. In my experience of working with such people, they will often speak of their building frustration in dealing with the other party such that they eventually lose control or become exasperated enough to be heavy-handed. In these situations where bullying is a byproduct of high frustration meeting poor emotional intelligence or skills, one usually sees high emotional honesty in the respondent and obvious remorse. In and of itself, one bully, misguided malcontent or authoritarian leader does not a culture make.

However, if the behaviour becomes the prevailing pattern of action and if people become sick from it, don't call it, make excuses for it, and are too scared to make mistakes or make decisions because of it, then it has become a feature of the culture in that workplace.

Bullying Versus Sociopathy

I have asserted that much bullying is unintentional. My experience has been that not many people seem to wake up each morning and say to themselves: 'I wonder whether I can psych someone out or mess with someone's head or make them feel really undermined or threatened today'. That degree of antisocial intent is not that prevalent.

Having said that, there is a degree of sociopathy in workplaces. Clinical research suggests that one in 100 men and 1 in 200 women are sociopathic (or antisocial in the old language). But it can really be the case that a sociopath can be a part of an organisational system and when they are, they can act like the addition of sour cream to a dish and rise to the top. How do we identify them? Even without a formal clinical diagnosis, we can infer things about people from what they say and do. While it's important to put sociopathy in perspective as occurring infrequently in the community, it is also important to realise that those who exhibit sociopathic tendencies may come across as highly intelligent, highly manipulative, and very charming and charismatic. They may say all the right things but be quite impervious to critical feedback. They can fly under the radar and quietly wreak havoc with staff, who start to wonder whether the problem is the sociopath or them. Staff can feel even more vulnerable if they believe the organisation actively supports the sociopath's work, results, or style. If that is the case, the only out for them at that point is to leave. Of course while I have mediated and investigated grievances where people appear to have intentionally sought to psychologically harm someone else, I have also observed countless individuals who through significant misguidance, clumsiness, or insecurity have lashed out and inflicted significant psychological and physical trauma on others.

Authoritarian Leadership Versus Authoritative Leadership

One of the most impressive leaders I know talks articulately about his belief in the importance of consulting with his people. I have seen him facilitate vigorous debates, and he does not appear to resent or be intimidated by disagreement. However, I have also seen him make a firm and unequivocal decision when he says he has to. He describes his approach thus: 'I'll consult to a point, and I am genuinely happy to have high bandwidth discussion, spirited debate, and have my people play devil's advocate. But when it's time for me to move on something, I move'. He holds people to account, deplores impulsivity and hypocrisy, and doesn't take too kindly to ill-conceived or unjustified criticism. He is an authoritative manager, but I don't believe anyone who works for him thinks of him as a bully. In fact, it probably won't surprise you to learn he is admired and respected by people at all levels in his organisation.

I worked with another client who became the subject of a bullying investigation, and I was asked to conduct some behavioural coaching after allegations had been substantiated against him. He was definitely not the sort of leader I have just spoken about. He became very angry during my work with him, attacking senior management and human resources for being wimpy and pandering to a few weak, lazy staff who in his opinion weren't prepared to do what it took to help the organisation succeed. He said the whole investigation was a sham, an ode to political correctness gone mad. In a moment of insight, he described himself as a tough, uncompromising manager with a commitment to excellence. From what I could gather, he may well have had a commitment to excellence, but he also committed numerous acts of aggression and intolerance, including berating staff in front of others and accusing his people of failing to respond in a timely manner to his requests. He e-mailed them late on Friday nights and when they did not reply until sometime on Monday, he would curse about how business had gone to the dogs and that no one took initiative anymore (except ironically and bravely to complain about him!).

He also denigrated a process that allowed his staff to complain about him to someone else meaning he was not the first to know of their discontent. He saw that as cowardly and their behaviour totally out of step with the 'Aussie way'. Well, based on my short description of him, who would have wanted to get alone in a room with him and give him feedback? (Any policy purported to be a good one must allow people to seek redress with someone other than the boss if the boss is the alleged perpetrator.)

Having said that, if the bully in our story were not so scary and unreasonable in his demands, chances are someone in that workplace may have been able to muster the courage to give him feedback directly. We might then have hoped that he had the good grace and the good sense to take that feedback onboard and exhibit more emotional intelligence. This was always improbable in this case because the aura this manager had given off was 'Do it my way, or suffer the consequences'. He had worked across the organisation in a number of roles for more than twenty years and had probably not changed a great deal except that people felt more empowered in a contemporary workplace to send up a flare. In this example, the individual was the culprit, but what had protected, tolerated, and justified his behaviour over time was a complicit culture: leaders who were prepared to accept the casualties in a highly competitive marketplace if they were to win the business war.

For some staff, bullying is not their preferred modus operandi, but they default to it when things are not going according to plan or they happen to possess low emotional intelligence including, as we say it in psychology world, poor impulse control. So, while some might be absolutely dismayed to be told they bully, they may unconsciously live by the credo 'When the going gets tough, the tough get tougher'.

How Bullying Conspires to Create Vulture Cultures

Bullying is undoubtedly a feature of many vulture cultures. Bullying costs, whether dressed up as authoritarianism, an 'ambitious change' agenda that demands employees continuously do more with fewer resources in less time, or a 'results focus' approach that borders on legal torture. Most profoundly, bullying costs because it is injurious to people's health, with all the associated implications for absence, productivity, and talent retention. Bullying also costs because people take their cues from the people around them. Bullying begets bullying in the same way that violence begets violence. If we consider Maslow's famous hierarchy of needs (from base physiological needs up to self-actualising needs), it stands to reason that people will find it difficult if not impossible to come to work each day and have the presence of mind and the intrinsic motivation to innovate (the new competitive advantage) if their basic needs for safety and security are not being met.

Chapter 7

Discrimination and Harassment

I n one round of diversity training sessions I ran for a government department a few years ago, I asked the group how old they were when they first realised life wasn't fair. One gentleman's hand shot up, and he announced he'd had that revelation at the tender age of three. I reflected that was fairly young and how impressive it was that he remembered it so readily (he looked to be around fifty). He told us that when he was three, his four-year-old sister kicked him. He pushed her back, and he got sent to the naughty corner! It was a humorous yet pointed example of the disappointment, indignation, and even rage we may feel when people are treated inequitably, particularly on grounds considered irrelevant in the circumstances. In this instance, the discrimination was seemingly on gender grounds, yet regardless of the prejudice that gives rise to the unequal treatment, the emotional reaction is almost always the same.

So while we know life isn't fair, we do have a wistful belief that good things should happen to people who deserve them and, as an extension of this, that bad things shouldn't be inflicted on those who don't.

Two damaging and prevalent ways to embody a vulture culture

characterised by toxicity, lack of ethics, poor management and low trust are to violate the rule of meritocracy or compromise the sacrosanct right to physical and emotional safety at work. To violate the rule of meritocracy — that the most deserving person gets the job — is to discriminate on unfair grounds. To intimidate, humiliate, or offend another at work based on protected attributes is to harass on unfair grounds. In a healthy culture, employees believe the best person will be rewarded with the opportunity and that people can come to work and go home in one piece, both physically and emotionally.

Exploding (more) Myths

As is my way, firstly, let's consider some myths that need to be exploded.

- **It's not (unlawful) discrimination if we don't choose an applicant because we think he or she will be a poor job fit.** This is both potentially true and untrue. A poor match on job-related criteria does give us the right to reject applicants, even if they belong to a minority group provided that they don't have the skills, knowledge, or other attributes required to do the job (determined on job-relevant criteria). However, we can continue to perpetuate unlawful discrimination if we decide that:
  - Only straight alpha males can be leaders in our organisations;
  - Only young, pretty females who can multitask can fill an assistant's role; or
  - Only workers of Asian origin should work on the night crew because our experience shows them to be hardworking and reliable.

In other words, we are permitted by law to make decisions on 'job fitness' based on objective criteria that don't rely upon protected attributes or perpetuate an otherwise subversive or homogeneous culture because it's easy or advantageous to do so.

- **Harassment is all about a power imbalance.** Some public figures, including our current Australian governor-general and a former sex discrimination commissioner, have declared harassment and sexual harassment as all about power. That may be true in many situations, but a junior person with no obvious contextual superiority may level an unthinking comment or even a supposed compliment at a senior person. That can still be harassment.

- **It was just a joke.** 'They' are trying to take all the fun out of the workplace. Unintentional harassment can create significant damage and lead to a pronounced lack of comfort or safety for the recipient of the attention. Intent is irrelevant. It is the impact that counts. Suggesting that some fictitious entity is trying to take the fun out of the workplace is a smokescreen for the desire to perpetuate bad behaviour or prey on people's fears. No one is trying to outlaw fun — only discriminatory or harassing treatment that disadvantages, intimidates, or harasses someone else. In a team environment, work life is fun when all parties are enjoying themselves.

- **It's only harassment (or sexual harassment) if it's intentional.** As with bullying legislation, what is assessed is impact, not intent. I dare say nobody gets in a car on any given day saying he or she plans to kill someone that day, but that's cold comfort to a victim's family after the fact. It is easier and more just to appraise someone else's behaviour than it is to attempt to read their intent; intentional or not, it can still hurt.

- **To constitute harassment (or sexual harassment), the behaviour has to be repeated or form part of a pattern of abuse.** Harassment is defined under Australian Equal Opportunity law as unwelcome, unsolicited attention that offends, humiliates, intimidates, or makes the workplace unpleasant. The offensive behaviour only has to happen once to constitute harassment. Similarly, sexual harassment is unwelcome attention of a sexual nature that offends, intimidates, humiliates, or makes the workplace unpleasant.

- **Harassment and sexual harassment legislation is no more than political correctness gone mad.** Some of us may not place huge stock in language that discriminates between the genders. My elder daughter is an actor in training, but she has no problem with the fact that Oscars are bestowed on best actresses and best actors, as there are more to go round! Some of us may not sweat it that the chairman of the board is a woman. I have met plenty of nonreligious employees who see no harm in the end-of-year Christmas party and can't see the sense in innocuous nomenclature like the 'end-of-year get-together thingy'. Many married female teachers at my younger daughter's school are proudly 'Mrs. Such and Such'. For all of these mild examples of apparent gender discrimination, there are also many vile stories and landmark cases of noxious treatment being perpetrated against staff by others who have callously intimidated, subjugated, stressed, abused, or propositioned people who have the right to 'quiet enjoyment of their workplace'. The solution to navigating our way through these issues practically and symbolically is respect for personal choice and respect for difference.

- **Any reasonable person receiving unwelcome attention must give the offending party direct feedback that the behaviour is offensive.** This is a cruel and immoral expectation as it effectively asks someone who may be highly intimidated to get alone in a room and give the offender (someone who doesn't care or hasn't bothered to work out that he or she is offensive or full-on scary) feedback. The further sinister implication of this flawed assumption is if feedback is not directly given, then the perpetrator has been wronged or that there is automatically no legitimate claim of discomfort or intimidation.

- **If it's not in writing, it's not real.** Perhaps this myth has morphed over the years from 'If it really concerns you, put it in writing, and I will treat this as a formal complaint to be investigated' to 'If you aren't prepared to put it in writing, I don't want to know about it!' Worse is another view shared with me some months ago by a manufacturing client: 'If it's not in writing, it never happened!' The recipient of the unwelcome attention usually wants it to stop. Indeed, the easiest, lowest cost, and least disruptive way to resolve these issues is for the recipient to decide he or she wants it to stop and for the offender to make it stop. Win/win! I have encountered many situations where the recipient of the attention brings it to someone else's attention to vent, to sort out feelings, or to get advice or other informal support to enable them to deal with it. The victim may want it to stop but may decide to stop short of invoking formal mechanisms to do so. Who could blame the victim for being reticent if these types of complaints have resulted in retaliation in the past?

- **If people aren't complaining, it can't be happening.** This myth is probably the ultimate delusion. Of course it can be happening. If staff are being discriminated against, harassed, or sexually harassed, they may feel significantly intimidated by the perpetrator and by the very real threat of backlash (the legal term is 'victimisation') to keep silent. In some cases, trust and expectations are so low (based on prior experience or company folklore) that people just shrug their shoulders, sigh deeply, think to themselves 'I told you so!' and stop asking for better treatment. Everything remains 'quiet' with no complaining while the dysfunctional behaviour continues.

- **Sexual harassment is perpetrated by men against women.** Sexual harassment is perpetrated by men against women, women against men, men against men, and women against women. The vast majority of external formal complaints are currently made by women against men for several reasons.

  - In many workplaces, women report to men. In those situations where the power imbalance is the catalyst for the unwelcome behaviour, by definition, it is likely to be the male who makes unwelcome overtures to the woman.

- An extension of this is that as we see more women appointed to roles previously occupied by men. They then become a minority group in those systems where before they were absent. There are some well-established risk factors for discrimination and harassment (and bullying), which include the presence of minority groups in the workplace. Thus, where the gender balance is still poor, women are vulnerable when the work culture and tolerance for difference has not caught up with reality.

- More women are involved in low-level service jobs than men. The master/servant mentality can cultivate a bad culture: for example, when men treat waitstaff and flight attendants more as slaves and maids than service providers, particularly in misogynistic groups or cultures or where the individual men have narcissistic tendencies (see chapter 12 on Lone Vultures).

- Men of many cultural origins, but certainly in Australian culture, would be too embarrassed to admit they find any overture from any woman unwelcome! Yet, logically speaking, why would they not have the same right to choose what they do and don't find welcome and by whom? I've heard many a man talk about this in my sessions only to be ridiculed by a colleague and aspersions cast on his sexuality for not wanting the 'harassment' to occur (which, if you think about it, is paradoxical as by definition, the behaviour has to be unwelcome to constitute harassment).

- Sex-based harassment and sexual harassment often coexist in workplaces. If women are more likely to be disadvantaged, picked on, or exploited for carer status or potential pregnancy, it is also more likely they will be objectified and sexually harassed. Men are also subjected to sex-based taunts ('Oh, he's a bloke — of course he can't multitask!'), and if he is surrounded by women who demean or ridicule him for being male, it is also plausible that he may be sexually harassed by them. Again, he may be too embarrassed to complain.

Real-life Examples

As we have already discussed, discrimination in the workplace isn't always some obvious act perpetrated by a bad person intent on causing damage. For example, when working in my second job out of university, I joined an executive search agency. Some of the applicant registration forms I was given to assess displayed symbols and stars: for example, a bright green asterisk accompanied a particular applicant's form. When I asked what that was for, the Practice Manager explained the applicant was of Asian origin. I asked why that was relevant to the application, and she replied with all the patience she could muster that some employers didn't want to interview candidates of particular races or national origins. I was completely taken aback but attempted to gather my thoughts. I then asked how we were expected to know which organisations had these biases. She enthusiastically explained, 'Those are what the yellow crosses are for'. Needless to say, I didn't end up staying at that job for very long. I am sure though that if I questioned the Practice Manager today over her secret coding system, she would argue that she wasn't being racist. She was catering to the clients' wishes, and as we know, the customer is always right.

Instinctively, most people think of (unlawful) discrimination as denying an opportunity to someone deserving by the application of an unlawful prejudice or bias. Unlawful or unethical bias can occur where people with particular attributes (including pre-existing relationships) are conferred a special advantage. In Vicky Ward's book *The Devil's Casino* about the rise and fall of Lehman Brothers, two nepotistic stories of 'friendly inbreeding' stand out. One was the appointment of Dick Fuld who was a wealthy client's grandson. He eventually rose to be CEO. The second was the recruitment of Jim Boshart by the infamously intimidating head trader Lew Glucksman. Boshart was reportedly six feet five inches tall, a former university basketball star and had a great jump shot. At the time of his employment the Lehman basketball championship featured a fierce rivalry between the bankers and the traders. The traders were down four games before Boshart joined the company (and the team). They went on to record twelve straight wins to finish first. Boshart rose to become Chief Administrative Officer.

A Case Study — Susan Dunn-Dyer vs. ANZ Banking Corporation

This case consolidated many of my mental models and beliefs about workplace culture. It occurred in the early 1990s whilst I was working with the ANZ Bank. I returned from maternity leave and asked for a challenging assignment. The bank was embroiled in a high-profile case of gender discrimination that was to change the course of my career: a young woman named Susan Dunn-Dyer sued the bank for gender discrimination under the unfair dismissals law after being passed over for two promotions and subsequently made redundant.

I was told I was the only person outside the Employee Relations team allowed to attend a day of the commission hearing, as the bank had decided that someone had to write a suite of modules to educate bank staff about appropriate and inappropriate workplace behaviour and the potential consequences. New unfair dismissal legislation had become effective in 1993; anti-discrimination legislation had been around since the 1970s, but it was gaining traction. The time to get serious about this 'EEO caper', as a manager called it, was well overdue. Months after the case had been determined and Dunn-Dyer had been awarded a $135,000 payout (which stood as a record in an Australian jurisdiction until the rumoured $1 million settlement in the David Jones vs. Fraser-Kirk case), a senior manager in Employee Relations told me at a bank Christmas party that if someone had just apologised to her about the treatment of women in that area at that time, it would 'probably never have gone that far'.

That comment had a profound effect on me: it was a powerful reminder of the importance of empathy for others' feelings and the defusing power of authentic validation. It set me on a professional path in conflict resolution and on a quest to understand what perpetuated angst for people long after many would have forgotten about it and let go.

As a psychologist, I was acutely aware of the grief often associated with loss, even when the loss is the loss of innocence and the importance of symbolic closure on events. The other issue for me at the time was how easy and natural it is for someone to put a negative frame around a decision (e.g., being 'unsuccessful' in winning a promotion must surely be due to gender grounds) if there is no trust in the workplace and processes and decisions are not transparent.

In the case of Dunn-Dyer she had no closure. Her case was in and out of the Human Rights and Equal Opportunity Commission for eighteen months. She represented herself and did not work in paid employment in that time. To my mind, her case became a mission to right an unacceptable wrong. Effectively, her payout would only have covered the loss of earnings over the two years she was unemployed, but that probably didn't matter much when one considered the passion and earnestness with which she appeared to follow her quest. She did countless fireside interviews and received a lot of media publicity, but it seemed clear that she craved vindication of a wrongdoing. She was brave at the time too, for many people remarked she had probably rendered herself unemployable after that as companies would be 'too scared to touch her'.

The most recent time I heard the same thing was in the aftermath of the Kristy Fraser-Kirk case. A treatment of any destructive workplace behaviour must be seen in the context of what the complainant risks by electing to complain. This further reinforces the nonsense of an assumption by a manager that if she isn't hearing about it, it can't be happening. Staff may have umpteen good reasons for being apprehensive to talk about a case of discrimination or harassment.

At that time, Dunn-Dyer was able to amass around 300 pages of evidence of what we would now call a 'hostile work environment'. That seemed to be enough to persuade the commissioner that women were likely to be disadvantaged in such a workplace if indeed they were otherwise not respected. So, the rationale for the decision was probably something like this: What are the chances that a woman working in a Hugo Boss-suit-wearing, three-mobile-phone-carrying, hairy-chested, golf-playing, testosterone-laden environment was going to get a fair go on promotion? You may not see an automatic connection, but the commission only had to decide on the balance of probabilities, which loosely translates to 'more likely than not'.

I almost hesitate to talk about the case because the culture of the organisation at that time was no different from that of many others who were pinged for similar things. But times do change and some of the credit for the bank's progress must surely be attributed to the transformational leadership of ANZ's former CEO, John MacFarlane, and his 'Breakout' initiative, which was all about changing the bank's core culture.

By working alongside ANZ's external lawyers at the time to learn about this 'EEO caper' and discovering a passion for workplace justice issues, I went on to develop a suite of modules to roll out across the bank to educate staff. The strategy adopted embodied the 'pool fence methodology,' to be discussed later in the book. We did not wait until someone else transgressed, only to haul them in front of a firing squad. Our rationale was to educate and then allow people to exercise their adult choice to toe the line or otherwise, while we were always prepared to call and remedy inappropriate behaviour.

A Case Study — Kristy Fraser-Kirk vs. David Jones Ltd.

When we transport ourselves from the Dunn-Dyer case to the Fraser-Kirk case, a more contemporary case of unprecedented media sensation, we see some disturbing themes in relation to discrimination and harassment. I say discrimination because the treatment at law of unwelcome negative attention directed towards an individual in Australian EEO legislation is perceived as a form of discrimination; that is, differential treatment by virtue of the unwelcome sexual attention. The fact that the attention allegedly offended, humiliated, or intimidated Fraser-Kirk is what constituted sexual harassment.

Here is what happened. Kristy Fraser-Kirk, a young marketing professional at the iconic upmarket Australian department store chain David Jones (DJ's), accused its CEO, Mark McInnes, of sexual harassment in August 2010. Fraser-Kirk sued McInnes and DJ's in the federal court for $37 million. In and of itself, this claim for damages was sure to attract extreme media attention. Debate raged for weeks between supporters and detractors about the wisdom in asking for such a large amount. Opinion was divided, but some of it was savage, which made Fraser-Kirk seem less like a victimised young woman seeking justice and validation and more like a woman hell-bent on a get-rich-quick scheme.

Sadly, some of the same themes I have observed on countless other occasions emerged. The media asked questions such as 'Why did Fraser-Kirk have an issue when other women came out in support of McInnes?' implying we should all have homogeneous feelings about what is or isn't offensive. Fraser-Kirk alleged the behaviour had been going on for years and no one in a position of authority did anything about it. She alleged the DJ's board knew that other women had been subjected to similar behaviour by McInnes but they had not felt safe to report it. She also alleged she told her general manager, who allegedly told her to say 'no' and that McInnes would then back off. McInnes, included in the Australian Financial Review BOSS magazine's Top 25 True Leaders in 2006, had doubled DJ's share price in the three years since his appointment. He was perceived to be a successful leader with a proven track record. The Age newspaper called him 'the darling of retail investors', and he was one of the youngest and most highly paid executives in Australia. Could this have been enough to make DJ decide to ignore what else came with the package until the scrutiny was so white-hot it felt compelled to cut the tangled parachute?

Fraser-Kirk's testimony during the case included her clinical psychologist's statement alleging she suffered from an adjustment disorder in the wake of the media frenzy and was reluctant to leave her home and be photographed. In reply the media were quick to reproduce photos of Fraser-Kirk seemingly happy and outside in public – on the other side of the world to Sydney in the Hamptons, New York! To make matters worse a high-profile fashion designer was then reported as saying she was extremely attracted to McInnes and he could have had her if he wanted her, thus objectifying herself and indirectly implying there was something wrong with Fraser-Kirk to have deemed the behaviour unwelcome.

While the media obviously plays an important public information role, and some are dedicated to the truth in investigative reporting, the innuendos about Fraser-Kirk and the depictions of her as money grubbing, attention seeking, or otherwise opportunistic were unsavoury examples of insidious behaviour designed to depict the alleged victim or subject as the potential villain. For some media commentators though, the fact that McInnes was powerful, charming, successful, and attractive did not invalidate Fraser-Kirk's right to determine what was or wasn't acceptable behaviour from colleagues in the workplace, however senior. In that light the $37 million claim for damages was a brilliant strategy designed to create a media furore and pressure DJ to settle ahead of a public hearing. And that is exactly what happened.

Watershed moments in history can catalyse discussion and opinion leading to positive change (including changes to legislation). However, what might have happened if Fraser-Kirk not been born into a well-to-do family with unequivocal parental support – her father was quite public in his support of her via social media – and what if her public complaint rendered her virtually unemployable thereafter? Would she otherwise have ever felt safe enough to mount her complaint?

How Discrimination and Harassment Conspire to Create Vulture Cultures

In the aforementioned examples, senior leaders allegedly perpetrated differential treatment that either significantly advantaged or disadvantaged one employee over others. For onlookers, this can have very destructive effects, as it can erode trust, morale, and engagement. It violates the two sacred principles we discussed at the beginning of our chapter. Firstly, the presumptive desire that good things should happen to good people and that bad things shouldn't; and secondly, that employees have the right to expect their employers will take seriously the moral and legal obligation to maintain employee physical and psychological health.

In keeping with our principles of what promotes and perpetuates vulture cultures, people can deny, avoid, excuse, or justify bad behaviour on the basis that it produces good results (e.g., a discriminatory practice that leads to victory and therefore bragging rights for Lehman Brothers in the basketball league) or that the end justifies the means (the CEO is too valuable to dispense with, so we just have to put up with his wayward behaviour or, at best, attempt to minimise any potential fallout). To top this off, we can see evidence in some examples of retaliatory behaviour against those who bring the message of bad culture and unacceptable treatment in the victimisation of complainants or their supporters. We see unwelcome attention meted out against those whose only crime is being different. In any case where the complaint brought is truthful and justified, is this victimisation not the ultimate perversion of justice?

Chapter 8

Incompetent Leadership

In essence, the preceding chapters have dealt with the dark side of leadership. As Barbara Kellerman points out in her 2004 book *Bad Leadership: What It Is, How It Happens, Why it Matters*, many people do not view tyrants, corrupt CEOs, and other abusers of power and authority as leaders. However, in its simplest form, leadership equals influence. These people most certainly have been influential — they stay in power and get others to do their bidding against all moral or ethical imperatives. They have used legitimate authority vested in them by the power of their position or the ability to punish and reward to shape other people's behaviour. We have talked extensively about the destructive force of individuals and systems of power used in this way, particularly when perpetuated by those leaders who would otherwise be the natural or designated custodians of culture.

As long as I can remember, people have exalted white, macho, and heterosexual alpha male leaders like Jack Welch, the former CEO of General Electric, in every respectable North American post-graduate program and business school. Welch was also arguably ruthless in terminating the employment of his bottom 10 percent of staff every year in his quest for excellence. He is one of the archetypal leaders lauded for the results they bring, with results defined narrowly as profit and shareholder return. A possible caveat regarding my characterisation of his ruthlessness is that he was up front and explicit about the likely fate of staff who didn't perform. Presumably, people joined the organisation knowing the risks. How easily, though, might we foresee in this methodology the sense of competitiveness that may have been engendered and worse, a perpetual climate of fear and an accompanying reluctance to talk about mistakes? These may also be the inevitable by-products of no-nonsense 'perform or perish'. Ironically, not only might some of the business schools have gotten it wrong by celebrating the wrong dudes, but also they themselves have received attention at times for the allegedly hostile and elitist culture they have created.

However, less attention has been focussed traditionally on those whose incompetence or ineptitude has either created a vacuum of power or authority such that staff run amok — that is, where the lunatics have taken over the asylum or where they do stupid stuff with disastrous results.

Exploding (more) Myths

As you've come to expect, first up are some myths that need to be exploded reflecting variations on the theme of incompetence.

- **You can't be liked and still be effective.** Early in his professional career, my husband, Fred, worked as Finance Manager for a multinational food manufacturer. As I'd been married to him for several years by then, it didn't surprise me when one of his staff told me on a visit that he was known as 'Mr. Nice Guy'. When I asked why, she said it was because he was fair and kind as well as competent. Fred happened to be reporting to a boss interstate, and the relationship was regrettably fractious from the start. The head office boss made unreasonable demands and wanted to compel Fred to drive his staff a lot harder. Fred came home a few months later and shared his boss's view of management with me. When Fred had asserted his boss was pushing the staff unreasonably, his boss said, 'You know you're a good manager when your staff hate your fucking guts'. Clearly, they were never going to see eye-to-eye. Needless to say, the relationship was exhausting, as Fred found himself in a position where he spent a great deal of effort advocating for his people and peddling harder to get done what he didn't feel he could ask them to do. He stayed a lot longer than was good for him because he didn't want to leave his staff in the hands of 'Mr. Sadly Misguided'. In contrast to Mr. Misguided, we might consider a man who by many accounts was an inspiring and visionary leader possessing wonderful people skills and charisma. John McFarlane, a native Scot, headed up ANZ Bank from 1997 to 2007. He was the leader at the time ANZ launched its major culture change program, 'Breakout', in 2000, which was designed to make ANZ a 'high performance values-driven organisation'. Both current and former staff have told me so many times how extraordinary it became to work at ANZ under his leadership. The bank appeared to flourish during his tenure, not only posting record profits but winning several customer awards reflecting high customer satisfaction whilst enjoying the highest employee engagement of any major company in Australia and New Zealand.

- **We're in charge, so we must know what we're doing.** Colleagues who worked under John McFarlane at the bank in the mid 1990s can attest that he was a charismatic yet genuine leader who sits in stark contrast to the leaders of the former era, one of whom, Will Bailey, oversaw the purchase of a beautiful estate in Flowerdale, Victoria. It was reportedly intended to be used exclusively as an executive retreat. With two full-time staff and numerous contractors, the property was renovated after purchase at a cost rumoured to be over $3 million, whilst country bank managers bitterly rostered the tea towel laundry duty to save a few dollars a week. After Will Bailey retired and Don Mercer took over as CEO, he decreed that Flowerdale be used henceforth as a training facility (since no one believed at that time that selling it would recoup anything close to its real value after the monumental capitalisation of the renovation). I was one of the first trainers allowed to run residential leadership courses there. When one big, burly country bank manager walked into the main building he was overcome with emotion at the privilege of being able to visit; others, not inclined to such generosity, shook their heads in disbelief at the immoral extravagance of such a purchase intended for use by a few people on only a few nights a year. The incompetence of those in charge demonstrated here is conceivably fuelled by avarice and a pronounced lack of empathy. It was also naïve in its lack of understanding of how the general public and the staff who serve under such managers are likely to perceive such actions. In *The Devil's Casino*, Vicky Ward writes about the Lehman Brothers executives at the time of the bankruptcy and 'the foibles of men, the corrosive influence of money and the dangers of hubris'.

- **What doesn't kill you only makes you stronger.** One argument espoused against organisations taking swift and decisive action against noxious behaviour is that we are creating a generation of wusses. In the old days, before bullying was publicised incessantly, people just 'copped it' and moved on; at least, that's what some outspoken critics of the ethics movement would have us believe. I don't think however there is any doubt that people can be differentially affected by the same stimulus. We see that in the schoolyard. Some kids laugh off bullying; other kids pretend to, but are genuinely affected. The fact is that some people seem remarkably unaffected by immense stressors and can live quite functional lives. I have seen this myself in having spent time with people who have come from war-torn countries (e.g., the Horn of Africa) and others who have made new lives for themselves post-World

War II: namely, Holocaust survivors. Few people in the know would argue that these people have remained unaffected by some of the worst atrocities we could fathom, but they seem to have been able to move on and live quite adaptive lives: working, living, laughing, taking joy in big and little things, and being able to trust, hope, and be happy. Others of us don't seem to be able to cope too well with the vicissitudes of life. Indeed, we regularly hear criticism of the 'youth of today', about whom it is said they've had it so good they don't cope with anything much! Clearly, personality plays a part, including the psychological concepts of self-efficacy, optimism, and locus of control, all of which can be measured on a continuum.

Yet, I take issue with this dangerous idiom that 'What doesn't kill you only makes you stronger'. This cannot and must not be taken as a given. Think of a plank of wood placed on someone's head. Instinctively, we are likely to want to push it off. A whole truckload dropped on someone might well crush him or her, despite the person's strength. There is little rhyme or reason to what could be the straw that breaks the camel's back, particularly if the straw is perceived by the camel to be a dense, heavy load of cement.

While some are seemingly unaffected *at the time*, we know clinically this is no guarantee they won't fall over later. The human mind is complex and not always rational. Many victims of bullying and other destructive workplace behaviour make new connections to old stimuli. Despite our complexity, we have only a very limited repertoire of responses to threat and danger. Fight or flight, either emotionally and or physiologically, is that common threat response. We can often recall the feel of that threat response as far back as our childhood, and that memory can be reawakened at a project meeting where people are threatening each other because of a missed deadline.

- **Incompetence via naïveté — If you walk out on me, you're weak.** Many clients who are victims of bullying or sexual harassment are often shocked at the intensity of their reaction to a particular event at work that seems so far away in time and place to their lives as children. They often experience what I explain to them is 'secondary anxiety' (basically, the fear of being fearful) and how unnerved they can be when otherwise highly functioning, competent individuals don't seem to be able to get themselves out of bed or defend themselves when being attacked. Their tongues cleave to the roof of their mouths, and they leave distressed or dispirited, wondering why they didn't have the gumption to stick up for themselves in the moment. However, we would not have survived as a species if we went toe to toe with everything or everyone who represented a threat, particularly if the person was bigger or stronger. Sometimes the tactical withdrawal is a good evolutionarily adaptive mechanism, but we're not necessarily proud of ourselves for doing it if we perceive our response as weak or think of all the things we could have or would have said (undoubtedly value judgments) if we had our time there over again. There is often that sneaking suspicion that if the other person seemingly got away with it, he or she might try it again.

- **Change is always good.** It is clear that the abilities to both manage and lead change have become core competencies. Change is here to stay, and it's getting faster and it can be for the better. Unfortunately though, the business case for change is not always well conceived. It is not always well planned in both the operational and psychological senses, and it is rarely well executed in maintaining the proper focus on the people and the message while the change is being introduced and then embedded. Leaders with low tolerance of ambiguity, poor patience, and negligible empathy will struggle to lead through challenging times. If they struggle in peacetime, then what are the chances they will have a level head in combat conditions? Some are good generals and can direct authoritatively and comfortably in crisis, but they may not always have the interpersonal skills to empathise or address resistance elegantly where change is anticipated and the process is protracted or unpopular.

Change leadership is as much about timing as it is about the tone and tenor of key change messages. If pressure ramps up and leaders become more introverted (i.e., less communicative), less patient, more self-interested, more buck passing, more focussed on the in tray, or more rigid, they will fail miserably to deliver on the change potential even if the reason for the change was a good one. Of course, to refer to ineffectual change leadership in this chapter implies that a failure to plan and execute well is a matter of competence or rather, incompetence. However, based on my consulting experience, we could just as easily include the issue of change leadership in the chapter that deals with unethical or corrupt practice.

Consider the following scenarios:

- Staff are excluded inappropriately from decision making (and, for example, this exclusion violates an enterprise agreement, other policy instrument, or agreed protocol),

- It might have been important to consult to develop more innovative solutions and ethical to pursue more 'owned' decisions, but this is seen as inefficient or tedious,

- Change leaders know they can't dress up a *fait accompli* as genuine consultation and don't want to be caught out,

- The change initiative itself is designed to produce unhealthy outcomes (e.g., create excessive workloads as a way of driving efficiencies), or

- The change rationale provided is dishonest (e.g., where particular staff have been targeted or downsizing is the inevitable, premeditated, but unspoken outcome of the change and the (main) reason for its instigation).

- **Incompetent Recruitment — I hired them; they must be good.** In chapter 2, I introduced Beryl, the long-serving and long-suffering executive assistant of the previous managing director. In the case of Beryl's new manager, he was determined to do it his way from the day he arrived. One symbolic and practical gesture to herald the idea that the winds of change were blowing was to change his personal assistant. Of course, another common occurrence with new hires is that if we've been the ones to endorse or select them, and if they prove to be a disaster, we often hold on far too long before we are prepared to step in, get involved, address the cultural issues, and if necessary, 'cut the tangled parachute' as that would amount to a drastic loss of face.

I discussed the perils of unlawful discrimination in chapter 7. But usually when people think of discrimination, they think discriminate *against*. In the phenomenon being discussed here, we are talking about discriminating *for*. At this point, I should talk about the theory of cognitive dissonance (CD). CD is an uncomfortable psychological state that occurs for us when we are presented with two contradictory beliefs. CD theory says we become mightily uncomfortable at the disconnect between the two beliefs and then have to find a way of dismissing one or reconciling the two. The pressure on the recruiting manager to convince himself or herself the person hired is really good is intense. What's the alternative? The manager is forced to look in the mirror and deduce any of the following:

- The applicant bluffed or deceived the manager in the selection process (so we're stupid or gullible),

- The recruiters were looking for the wrong attributes at the time of selection (so we're misguided, unprepared, or stupid again),

- They failed to consider what would and wouldn't work

(in other words, we have no conceptual or strategic nous), or

- They've wasted company money on a bad hire, and it could be expensive and tedious to make good on the mistake (read that as I'm stupid, and fixing it could be expensive and tedious).

We also know that the more often we are forced to defend someone or something, the more we can become fused to that belief or have to back down. If many people have complained and managers are defensive in backing a staff member, they could become even more closed to the feedback. So either way, to accept the person was a bad hire is to say we were foolish and duped, stupid and unplanned, or nonstrategic and naïve at best. None of those are complimentary labels. For other contextual reasons, they may be inclined to adopt the Stephen Stills methodology and 'love the one they're with' even if they realise they made a bad hire, as someone else could always be worse.

There could also be a freeze on employment such that the new person would not be replaced. The leader could be fearful of industrial retaliation or share price impact if someone in a key role were rumoured to be a dud. They could realistically be worried the news would rebound on them and their decision-making credibility. They could hold the belief the incumbent isn't great, but having no one would be worse. In their inspired decision making, they may have bestowed a fixed-term contract on the schlemiel, in which case they could have to face the prospect of paying someone out to do nothing much in particular.

If we contemplate more conspiratorial reasons for clinging to life with a bad hire, it could also be that nepotism was at work in the first place and that the new hire 'has something' on the person responsible for hiring. In one organisation I worked with recently, the staff were so dismayed a particular individual was allowed to survive and thrive they speculated often whether indeed the person kept on had some dirt on the boss.

The team had no respect for the dud manager or the CEO for allowing the person to continue to make poor decisions, undermine good culture, burn clients, and disillusion good staff into leaving. Mistakes like this one inevitably cost the organisation big time. To misquote Groucho Marx, staff could adopt the attitude that 'I don't want to belong to a club that would have that schlemiel as a member!'

- **A little bit of nepotism or favouritism is okay.** Another example of both discriminating *for* and the lunatics taking over the asylum can be found in the selection decision made to provide an (unfair) advantage for friends or family if they are not perceived to be deserving. One could argue in the best spirit of equal opportunity that if this candidate is the best person for the job, he or she should be given the opportunity and not disadvantaged unfairly *just* because of the relationship. As an EEO practitioner myself, I will not argue with such equity logic. However, I have seen bad blood created so often where perceived lightweights get a leg up from someone keen to advantage them when others would say the candidates were not deserving. It is the perception as much or more than the reality of their 'dudness' that kills morale. Working in heavy manufacturing in my early consulting years, it was not uncommon to meet several men on the shop floor with the same surname. For every person I met who complained that a particular family had the inside track, others said some of those who had come to the business were highly skilled and had a great attitude and viewed the company as their own company with a lot vested in having it succeed (because it employed many family members). In other words, just being related or close should not be grounds to advantage or disadvantage anyone, but common sense must prevail when ratifying the company's organisational chart.

Case Study — He's Heavy (going); He's Your Brother-in-Law

A few years ago, I worked with a team whose senior manager branded them as significantly underperforming. In our prebrief, the team presented quite fearfully. I observed a lot of animosity between them and their first line supervisor. The senior manager made the unusual decision to absent herself from the workshop, explaining it was important for them to have time to work together without her interference. The vibe in the room was edgy, and I could tell they were skirting the issues of what they really wanted to discuss. I reached out to a couple during the morning tea break. They made it clear they didn't have a great relationship with their senior manager, who was constantly implying in meetings that they weren't doing their job. They felt she was a patsy for the supervisor. When I asked why they couldn't go to her about the supervisor, they replied because he was the senior manager's brother-in-law and they came to work together by car each day! In fact, the couple of times they alleged they had stood up to their supervisor, the senior manager had been cold and aloof with them for days, so they were sure he discussed everything with her. It's very hard to be emotionally honest when there is no trust.

One could argue that the decision to place the two family members in positions of authority, one reporting to the other in the same division in the same organisation, was foolish at best or subversive at worst. Where does incompetence morph into unethical behaviour or even corruption? This was not just about good old-fashioned nepotism or what we might call 'jobs for the relos' (relatives). Assuming people knew the connection — and this team was in no doubt at all about that — someone in a pay grade higher than those two decided the idea was okay some time before and didn't check in to see whether this was working for the staff. Instead, Human Resources and I were asked to wave some invisible magic wand to 'fix' a group and make them more productive when their morale was in their bootstraps, trust with management was rock bottom, and their most basic needs were not being met. They did not feel safe.

Incompetence via Neglect

Sometimes leaders aren't incompetent because they are doing the wrong thing. Sometimes they are incompetent because they *don't do anything.* They are just plain absent. The big sign on the door says 'Gone Fishing'. The leader is guilty by virtue of neglect. If what is going on is bad enough and costly enough, it can go beyond neglect to plain negligence.

Returning again to the example of loyal, devoted Beryl, the former personal assistant to a senior manager who retired, the senior manager's replacement had someone else in mind for Beryl's role. He clearly ostracised her, nitpicked her work, made his disapproval clear, and constructively dismissed Beryl. He made her life at work so disagreeable that she went out on stress, never to return.

On the face of it, this was the senior manager's wrongdoing. But his peers and an executive manager remained silent. They had far more of a rich history with Beryl than the incumbent manager. No one vouched for her, stuck up for her, offered to place her on his or her team, or read between the lines about the behaviour being doled out on her. The faulty beliefs were probably along the lines of the following:

- 'The new manager is entitled to choose his own PA',
- 'He must know what he's doing or no one would have recruited him',
- 'It's not for me to meddle in something that's not my business',
- 'I wouldn't want someone telling me what to do either', or
- 'I don't want to get a new senior manager offside early in our relationship', etc.

Even if the peers did not feel comfortable challenging this manager directly, where was the executive manager? Not surprisingly, she was earning a reputation for being a hands-off manager, vesting too much autonomy in her staff, which in this instance translated to unacceptable, unchecked behaviour. Herein lies the tension. No senior manager wants to be oversupervised. To do so can breed a culture of compliance, absence of initiative, and burnt-out martyrs. The executive was always going to be walking a tightrope when trying to dictate terms to her new senior manager. But we can put a frame around this that says the following:

> *You are my senior manager. I trust you to run your part of the business but just know the way we do things around here is just as important as what we do and achieve.*
>
> *I would like to think that Beryl is given every fair and reasonable opportunity to prove herself as a personal assistant to a brand new boss and that might take some patience, some coaching, and goodwill on your part so she knows she's being given a genuine chance. If it doesn't work out, we owe it to Beryl to facilitate her move elsewhere with dignity and grace. After all, she has given us twenty years of loyal and devoted service, and if she's not quite up to par, then we've failed to manage it.*
>
> *For what it's worth, my observation is she does her best work when she is appreciated and feeling secure, so be gentle with her, get to know her, and give her the best chance to succeed. Be honest with her about what you need and expect so she has all the information with which to make quality decisions. If she 'makes a blue,' I would expect you to let her know, but respectfully so. Thanks.*

In this instance, the incompetent executive manager has failed to monitor what's going on, missed an opportunity to begin the ethics narrative with her new direct report, and assumed too much about the senior manager's fair-mindedness.

Incompetence via Exaggerated Self-Interest

There has been much discussion in the media the past few years, starting in 2006 and reaching fever pitch in the wake of the global financial crisis, about the corruption of executive leadership reflected in behaviours, the level of remuneration, and a lack of empathy and ethics. (See chapter 5.) However, on a smaller scale, some managers, entrusted with the responsibility to lead by example and to demonstrate care, can be motivated by self-interest in a way that reflects blind stupidity as much or more than good old-fashioned hubris. We can be scathing of politicians, as an example, if we believe they are motivated by looking good, living the glamorous life, and misspending taxpayer money when they should be serving their constituents. One only has to monitor the blogosphere and hear staff talk with contempt about shallow senior managers who flit from function to function, creating opportunities to hobnob with celebrities, fill mantelpieces with framed photo opportunities, and do lunch in all the best restaurants.

I have seen a classic case of this at a nonprofit organisation. The staff's view of the CEO was that she spent much of her time trying to make herself look good. Her mispronunciations (yet she hated people talking 'jargo') and confused usage of words was legendary. They said she was perennially big-noting herself, refusing to listen to advice, and taking credit for others' work. They were scornful of her decision to hire a permanent driver (while the nonprofit's clients were below the poverty line) and reportedly failed to act on several public relations disasters that haunted the organisation. By all accounts, she wasn't up to the job, which it would appear she understood herself. On one occasion, at the end of the workday in the presence of colleagues, she adjusted her silk wrap before heading off to the opera with clients and allegedly shook her head with a smile and said, 'Gee, life's good. I can hardly believe I'm here'. A few months later, she wasn't, but only after virtually the whole senior management team, including some regarded as extremely talented, had departed in disgust.

PART THREE

'Shifting Culture, Culling Vultures'

Chapter 9

Intervening in a Self-Perpetuating Predatory System

Twenty years of consulting have led me to believe that one individual *can* disrupt a system, but a vulture culture is a system whereby disruptive, debilitating, unethical, or toxic behaviour is *perpetrated* or *enabled* by the system.

A counsellor friend shared a story with me a few years ago that illustrates this in a very different system to that of a business. She told me of a family that presented with a very bright six-year-old who was acting out. He was violent at times, belligerent, attention seeking, and disruptive: in short, a real handful. The parents went to my colleague to have Billy (not his real name) sorted out after he had found some matches and allegedly tried to set fire to his sister's hair. In the first session, he sat there quietly while his parents recounted a tale of woe about what it was like trying to raise Billy. He sat stony faced and impassive, occasionally blinking hard but absorbing every disparaging word. After a short while, when it became clear there was not going to be an upside to their story, my colleague asked the young boy whether this was an accurate summary of some of the challenges in the family. He said that it was. The counsellor asked to speak with him alone, which shocked the parents, but they reluctantly agreed, particularly after reminding themselves that he was the problem.

When they were alone, my colleague asked Billy how it felt to hear those things. He admitted it was rough but added it was all true. He also admitted he didn't enjoy getting told off all the time and excluded from family time by being sent to his room. The counsellor then asked him why he did those things if they weren't fun. He looked at her hard for several moments, was about to speak, and then hesitated. She quietly told him she would not share his answer with anyone else unless he let her. His voice cracked as he told her he did all those naughty things to keep his parents together. He wasn't sure they loved each other much anymore, and he didn't want to grow up without one of them in his life, which is something his closest buddy at school had to do. With permission, my colleague shared this with the parents (but without Billy in the room), and this became the catalyst for them to work on their relationship. Billy's behaviour was merely the presenting manifestation of a 'system' in crisis.

In this powerful and provocative true story lies the premise on which all our work on organisational strategies is predicated. The keys to creating and sustaining better organisational health and eliminating counterproductive workplace behaviour in the service of innovation, work productivity and quality, profit, morale, job satisfaction, retention of talent, business reputation, and risk management lie in a holistic multifaceted approach that may include important work to be done at the organisational, team, and individual levels in the system.

In Billy's case, his behaviour met a need: his acting out served a purpose for Billy and his parents. It was the same need for the two sets of parties: to provide a *shared* focus for the parental relationship and to distract them from the stuff going on between them that wasn't working. Billy's challenging behaviour was also a way to validate the tension in the family, and it prevented family members from having to look in the mirror and see problems (in this case anger, resentment, and depression) in themselves. Some factors that enabled the continuation of Billy's behaviour were the game playing and point scoring that existed between the parents and the boundaries that the parents did not consistently enforce. None of this is to say that Billy's behaviour wasn't extremely difficult. He could have found subtler and less damaging ways to manifest insecurity and give his parents something in common. I am not trying to excuse or justify Billy's challenging behaviour or to suggest this wasn't a real burden for the parents. But at the end of the day, this boy was just six years old, and his parents were subconsciously duplicitous in Billy's acting out by failing to address the underlying causes, allowing the misery to continue.

Our Major Premise on Shifting Culture

To effect a cultural shift in an organisation, its leaders must focus on the long-term and short-term through *the formulation of organisational values* and collaborating and communicating how those *values are to be demonstrated in everyday action at work.*

Every existing organisation has a legacy culture and a current workforce. I would not automatically advocate a wholesale change in staff as the only way to get things back on track. And indeed, moving a toxic person elsewhere in the organisation is wimping out. I've even heard executives talk about 'promoting people up and out of the way'. Much good work can be done to change culture, but it requires some vital ingredients. They set the framework for the successful execution of culture change at the level of the organisation, the team, and the individual.

Signs That We're Serious — Lofty Ideals or Lived Values?

Companies can (and frequently do) have well-publicised values sitting on high-quality board behind anti-glare Perspex on a swank boardroom wall. They might also make little novelty gadgets, launch campaigns, draft cheat sheets, and print them on stress balls, mini calendars, and laminated cards and appliqué them to staff uniforms as reminders. But how do we know whether any of our cutesy memory joggers about company values are actually working? Are these organisations living their mission statement?

There are three prime indicators of accountability for good culture:

1. The extent to which any of the inappropriate or 'below the line' behaviours are ever actually *committed*,

2. Whether they are 'called' if committed, and

3. Depending on the severity, even if they are *called*, are they *'consequenced'*?

Failure to take action is often defended, justified, or explained by any or all of the following:

- 'I had no idea!'
- 'It wasn't that bad!'
- 'I haven't got time'.
- 'The person is going through a hard time'.
- 'But the person is my drinking buddy' (or variations on that theme).
- 'I do worse myself'.
- 'Someone else did worse last week and we did nothing about that. We need to be consistent!'
- 'The person will just call in the union'.
- 'The rest of the team won't like me'.
- 'The rest of the team will think I'm too tough'.
- 'The rest of the team will think I have no sense of humour'.
- 'If I take offence, the rest of the team will think I'm too soft'.
- 'No one made a formal complaint'.
- 'I don't want to involve Human Resources'.
- 'I don't want my manager to know I haven't got control of my people'.

- 'But this person does such great work. One has to take the good with the bad'.
- 'But this person brings in so much money. I can't afford to lose him or her'.

That's a pretty realistic yet formidable list, and I haven't really tried all that hard to list as many excuses as I have heard over the years.

Essentially, these 'dexefications' (defences, explanations, and justifications, with due credit to my colleague Allan Parker) can be collapsed into a few categories. What they all have in common is that they are all uttered by a leader who has shirked — even abdicated — responsibility, thereby damaging the fabric of the organisation. Whether the perpetrator falls into the bucket of too powerful, too profitable, too productive, or too popular, that person is certainly too protected and, in some cases, actively promoted.

With all of these good reasons for maintaining the status quo, our experience tells us that success in disrupting and recreating culture requires a number of critical elements working in parallel. Simply put, disrupting the system and embedding any attitudinal or behavioural change requires courage, fierce resolve (genuine motivation, commitment, and tenacity), legitimate authority (which includes credibility), a 'burning platform' or compelling reasons or drivers for change, a success blueprint for what 'good' or 'great' looks like, talented people, the allocation of time and money, and the understanding it *will* take time.

And it goes without saying that all this needs to be driven by courageous and authentic leaders.

Critical Success Factors
Courage
An existing vulture culture remains self-perpetuating unless there is real change. Sometimes, even in horrific situations we can never understand, people would rather maintain the status

quo, so a decision to disrupt the system and face the heavy push-back that may come requires real courage and 'stickability'. Indeed, changes can result in some industrial or employee relations outworkings, so you need to be brave enough to forge ahead when heavy hitters might be telling you what you want to do is 'dangerous' or high on reputational risk, particularly in an organisation with a low appetite for risk or political exposure.

Genuine Motivation, Commitment, and Tenacity

Courage on its own is not enough: people must want change. The team or department must decide that they yearn for something else and are willing to do what it takes to create a new history. This resolve will be tested, so it must reflect genuine intent to start with. In the short term, things could get worse, so the change leader must have resolve to weather the storm. We know from goal-setting motivational literature and practical experience that part of the ability to stay motivated (in tough times) hinges on whether *we truly believe it can work*.

So what else needs to be in place for people to sustain their belief?

Legitimate Authority

The person or people committed to leading the change must have some serious credibility and authority. They have to be able to demand a better working life, mobilise and deploy assistance, direct people to be involved, and prioritise this work over other work if people are time poor or under pressure. They have to be able to make tough decisions. That is not to say that other members of a team or a system may not be able to play a constructive role, but if the leadership aren't behind the culture revolution, it will fail — particularly since some leaders probably have protected the toxicity and allowed it to become a feature of 'the way things are done around here'. Time and again, well-intentioned people with insufficient clout are the appointed or self-appointed change leaders. This is commonly the case with well-meaning, highly qualified Human Resources personnel who, at the end of the day, can only give advice or make recommendations. Senior leadership can thwart them overtly or via subterfuge, procrastination, or avoidance. So HR may not have the decision-making or gate-keeping clout. The company's board may be too far removed to be able to control the consistency of the message. The CEO may well be senior enough but may not have the active support of all the lieutenants, and so the message dissipates as it permeates the layers. Local team leaders may do wonders with their teams at a local level and then find they've been left out in the cold as other organisational gatekeepers (including their own manager) frustrate their access or circumvent or isolate them.

A Burning Platform for Change

Driver One — Crisis as a Big Impetus for Change.
Sometimes there needs to be an overwhelming, inescapable rupture in the system that compels people to act. People may need a crisis or some irrefutable evidence of the cost or risk of allowing things to stay as they are such that they understand they cannot ignore it.

To revisit the example of Billy's family at the start of this chapter — Billy attempted to set fire to his sister's hair and this threat of real harm to a member of the family too young to defend herself was the catalyst for his parents to present at counselling. Admittedly, they got more than they bargained for, as they found themselves implicated in the problems and therefore in the solution. And so it is often with workplaces as well. Some big-ticket critical incident catapults people into movement or, more likely, shocks them out of their compla-cency. They discover some inescapable evidence of the fact that the world as they thought they knew it isn't that world or is a world no one can inhabit anymore.

Case Study — Part of the Problem"

A high-profile government project of enormous import was struggling for months. It was an open secret that the project was massively behind on milestones and on budget. Staff were stressed. There was lots of unbridled hostility and destructive conflict, chronic absenteeism, and illness. Other teams and departments frequently referred to the project team as incompetent and dysfunctional even though there were some individual superstars in the bunch. The board searched for a top-flight project manager with a proven track record and convinced him to pull the project together. The only thing staff had agreed on for months was that this person was a top appointment. Some expressed quiet optimism things might turn around.

Three weeks after he started as project head, he left. He said that as badly as things had been painted, the situation was far worse than described. He didn't want to expend all his time and energy building from scratch when there was so much exciting work to be done. The resignation of this individual shocked and embarrassed the team. They woke up to the realisation that something had to change. In the project manager's departure, they finally recognised they were a big part of the problem and therefore the solution. Real change had to happen.

Typically, one needs to establish a true sense of urgency *without* creating a fake emergency, which can either erode trust or have people become habituated to the drama and stop reacting. One key motivator for change is the experience of considerable pain. For example, an organisation is named and shamed in the papers, so it launches a review. A government official is publicised for allegations of reprehensible behaviour, which then becomes the catalyst for the launch of an investigation. The media asserts an emergency services organisation was derelict in its duties in the wake of a community crisis, which may spark a judicial enquiry or royal commission.

But even if there's pain, senior people may refuse to acknowledge it. The idea that something bad is happening on their watch may be too scary to confront. Perhaps they feel powerless to do anything about it or were never told things are as bad as they are. In some ways, the most senior people in an organisation can become 'prisoners of their own elevation'. They may be scary dudes, so no one wants to displease them. They are gatekeepers to others' success, so people may not want to displease them. They may fear losing their bonuses or being disgraced in front of the board, so they bury their heads in the sand or spend a lot of time and energy throwing sand over the whole thing to cover the crevasse underneath. They may not take too kindly to being told things aren't working and be inclined to shoot the messenger. As noted above, they may be formidable or intimidating themselves, so asking staff to stand up to them and tell them some truths they've done their best to ignore or condone may not be realistic. In this case for change to occur you need to amass significant evidence of the pain to convince leaders of its existence.

To shock people out of their denial, complacency, and duplicity, you may have to provide irrefutable proof of the fact that things are not as they seem and can't afford to stay that way. People's innate *protective* drive is galvanising their denial. You have to counteract that with the costs and risks of keeping things as they are to get their protective drive going in another direction, such as fear of adverse publicity or project failure if they *don't* fix the culture. The ethical way to do that is to *first* establish evidence for the need to change and *then* launch the intervention. We know how it can feel when we see governments or companies we believe embark on programs motivated solely by self-interest and then try to find or manufacture evidence or a rationale for what's been initiated after the fact.

Proof may come in the form of 360-degree feedback, exit interviews, grievance findings, employee opinion survey results that segment areas and identify hot spots, evidence of theft, sharp drop in sales, substandard product quality, or high levels of absenteeism or presenteeism (as a symptom of poor culture or as a cause). HR are often a great partner in amassing evidence but butt heads with those who still don't want to change or don't have the means or the self-belief to sustain motivation. Individual personnel may also be deficient in the influence skills required to sell the impetus for change.

Driver Two — Majestic Possibilities as a Big Impetus for Change. Sometimes we are moved to change things in life for the best of reasons. We can be motivated to move for the promise of what lies ahead. Contrast the person who has a heart attack and resolves to give up smoking once and for all for fear of dying with the overweight person who sets a goal to lose 10 percent of her body weight and then finds she is motivated and confident to reset her goal because she is looking and feeling better and her self-belief has increased. Or the person who runs his first half-marathon and is so exhilarated as he crosses the finish line that he then resolves to work towards the big one — the 42 kilometres. The choice to move in the smoker's scenario has been referenced in literature on motivation as the *protective* drive: the motivation to reduce pain or to prevent something bad from happening. The second has been referred to as the aspirational *drive:* the motivation to close the gap between where we are and where we could be.

We do not dwell in this book on the organisation or the team that sees competitive advantage or even better morale in continuing to work on permeating its values through the organisation — these values-based organisations are very unlikely to constitute vulture cultures. Having said that, these frameworks and methodology allow for the harnessing of both the protective drive and the aspirational drive. We routinely tap into the pain to be alleviated but infuse our strategies by imagining everything we stand to gain by doing it well. My gifted speaker buddy,

Allan Parker, who, as a man of sixty, is working towards qualifying for the Hawaiian Ironman, can describe in vivid detail how it will look, feel, smell, and taste to churn through the water in pursuit of his dream. The goal is infused with an intoxicatingly positive emotion to keep him motivated as he hits the Sydney surf in the wee hours of the morning to practise.

Change Leader Talent — The Right Stuff in the Right Staff

Let's say the leader has a compelling need to change and is sincere about wanting to change the tide. The leader needs to bring together the right people to do this. An obvious business partner or trusted adviser is the HR practitioner, but it's very hard for HR to do this on their own. Inasmuch as they are in the organisation and paid a salary, they are part of the system. They have to maintain ongoing relationships with people, so taking others on requires real skill and elegance. If the leaders don't want their advice and support, they will likely tell them. Depending on their skills and background, they may or may not be able to pull it off. Some are brilliant at support, training, or strategy, but not necessarily change management or courageous conversations. You can bet that if their own team is dysfunctional and there is little emotional honesty in the way they work together, they are not likely to be much help to you.

However, I find that HR people are generally not accorded the respect they deserve because of the snobbish cultural norm between those who bring home the bacon to the organisation (the 'hunter-gatherers') and those who support, enable, and facilitate outcomes (disparagingly viewed as the 'hangers-on'). Great HR practitioners are worth their weight in gold and often get a bad rap because they will slow down or examine a process and tell us we have not been procedurally fair such that we must go back to the drawing board. In so doing, HR can be seen as obstructive when they are really trying to mitigate risk and promote fairness and equity. They can be a wonderful business partner who will also be looking for signs of real commitment and courage in the leaders with ultimate accountability for culture and with the authority to drive the necessary change.

A Vibrant Picture of Success — A Blueprint for What 'Good' Looks, Feels, and Sounds Like

People need to know what it is they are expected to do. They have to have a clear understanding of what the alternative way of 'being' actually is, and it is critical that this is done at the feeling level and at the behavioural level. One can say 'I care about world peace'. But what am I doing about it? I can say I care deeply about respecting the individual. But does my behaviour reflect that? I might bang on about child poverty, but in a practical sense, what catalyses action if I don't know where to start?

Time and Resources

In my business every now and then a prospective client sees something I have done in the media, gets a referral via word-of-mouth from a generous client, or does a Google search on organisational psychologists and finds me. We have a meeting at which the prospect openly (or cryptically) tells me about some issues he or she has in the organisation: issues that may have gone on for a long time, been debilitating, resulted in some negative publicity, compromised productivity or profitability, produced an unflattering employee opinion survey, or resulted in stress claims, chronic absenteeism, or one or more talented people leaving. (I am sure you get the picture.) Then, the prospect asks whether a one-day team workshop should do the trick. Of course, the short answer I give to the prospective client is 'no' nor would I be prepared to run it! They are not the sort of client anyone needs. Worse than the meagre amount of time or money they are prepared to allocate is the prospect's lack of spine in owning his or her naïveté or lack of motivation to fix things. Even if the prospect is sincere and really wants to fix it (I can't condemn the person for not being an expert in culture change methodology) all this person really wants to do is to tinker around the edges. Being serious means finding money and pushing other things aside to make space for a shift in mindsets and behaviours *and* for some healing to take place. That takes time.

Patience

Shifting an organisation takes time: months and years. People regress even when they're motivated. Some people fight and expend a lot of energy shoring up resistance and garnering support. As we've discussed, the system is self-perpetuating. Something about what is happening meets needs, so moving from that into discomfort and destabilisation is not always done willingly.

Beyond that, as things start to shift, it can take a while before the rhetoric catches up with the behaviour. Some can still talk nostalgically or critically about a company based on what was, rather than what is, or what it is becoming. So the organisation can be like the movie star who buys into their own publicity. It can continue to mythologise about the past as if it were the present.

People have to look for signs of change to notice them. I call this the 'window blinds ad' phenomenon. When does our brain filter pick up on detail it previously ignored? When there's a need. That's when we finally notice the countless television advertisements for vertical window blinds: when we're in the market for them. To see shifts in mindset or behaviour, we have to be looking for them. If we don't want the change, we will look for continued evidence that the world as we know it has *not* shifted. The critical thing is to be both realistic and optimistic at the same time, not to lose heart or resolve, and to continue to communicate about where we're going, why, and what it will look like when we get there, without becoming demoralised when it takes us longer than we hoped.

Maintaining Holistic Focus — The Seduction of Fixating on the Squeaky Wheel

The final critical success factor is an unswerving belief in the need to change the system at the highest as well as at the lowest level. Every staff member is part of a system. The culture is the social structure: it is the unwritten ground rules of how the organisation operates, what it stands for, and what it lives and dies by. Organisations can do well to make those things explicit. It's not fair to ask people to live by a code or rules without letting them know what these rules are. It would be as ludicrous as changing the rules of international football in the off season, failing to communicating the changes to the clubs in the league, and then awarding a penalty kick or red card when someone messed up during the actual game. Making the rules explicit is not an automatic guarantee everyone will live by them, but there's no hope that people will all follow the same path if it isn't mapped for them.

Once the framework is enunciated, the next step is to set people up to win with the knowledge and the skills to be able to play well and within the rules of the game and to ensure that is underpinned by real motivation to do so. I have seen coaches go about the business of radically reengineering the game plan or shifting people into dramatically different roles. Players can forget the game plan and then lose the match, angering their supporters. The best coaches will talk afterwards about the fact that players stuck to their structures and held their positions as the most obvious manifestation of success. In other words, they recognise that they are a culture in progress. At that point in their evolution, worrying about the week-to-week results is foolish. They are in it for the long haul and expect to see the fruits of their labour over time. Obsessing about the minutiae when they are building a new psychosocial climate for their business is distracting them from what matters most at that time.

Having said that, leaders *cannot* go to sleep at the wheel on individual perpetrators. Once they have drawn a line in the sand and published and educated on what is and isn't acceptable, they have licence to act on individual transgressions. They should not become disheartened and lose resolve over individual transgressions because they can get some of the people to do the right thing eventually, but not all of the people all of the time and straight away!

Remember also what we are doing here is disrupting the system, so we may well get some chaotic or highly resistant pushback in the short to medium term as people desperately try to cling to an old reality and convince themselves that life as they knew it isn't really over. Of course, any hypocrisy in saying one thing and doing another will be met with disillusionment and sometimes rage. However, we have to stand for something: that's the big picture. We then have to recruit, select, manage, motivate, and discipline each staff member against it: that's the small picture. The two dimensions constantly interact and sometimes collide.

Now that we have advocated for a holistic solution and showcased the necessary precursors to successful organisational culture change, let's explore methodologies for intervening at the organisational, team, and individual levels.

Chapter 10

Strategies for Culture Change at the Organisational Level

It is well documented that children growing up in a home without rules and appropriate consequences for not following rules can be chaotic and rudderless. They may not want boundaries, rules, or discipline, but we know they need it. Ask family therapists, and they will tell you that it isn't essential that parents get it right every time, but it is vitally important in a two-parent household or shared parenting arrangement that they are consistent with each other. As children grow, it is appropriate to relinquish some of the power and autonomy to them to demonstrate their capacity to self-regulate and flourish in a supportive environment. And they will flourish more in a relationship where they are safe, well, engaged, and intrinsically motivated rather than dominated by rules of what is or isn't acceptable. Thus, rules and boundaries are important in setting a minimally acceptable level of behaviour. The inspiration comes in living according to values as a key to a mindful and contented life. We all visit homes characterised by love and respect. This likely has been created by values instilled and modelled around showing respect and care for others, not a rule that stipulates one shall not raise one's voice above 20 decibels.

Therefore, the first major thrust of our organisational strategy to prevent and defeat a vulture culture is a platform that includes a values narrative and a policy regime working in harmony. The second major thrust is dedicating ourselves to setting people up to win by educating them around this so that they know what's right and can deliver on it. The third is embedding the shift in culture and resisting the temptation to focus all the energy on the offending individual, as we just may not get the change we want. We explore each of these elements below.

Strategy Step One — The Ying and the Yang — Values Narrative and Supporting Policies

The first part of our methodology is a big picture consisting of a framework of values operationalised in action as clear identifiable behaviours. In the previous chapter, we identified two major drivers of behaviour: the aspirational drive and the protective drive. Creating a values narrative represents the aspirational piece, as we are always striving to realise these values in everything we do and in each transaction with someone else. However, this must be supported by work done at the protective end of the continuum: a minimum set of acceptable behaviours in the form of a suite of policies that spells out the rules of engagement and what happens if people don't meet the minimum standards.

While policies are critical, we can't afford to let policies do all the talking. Unless it is a reward and recognition policy, I have never seen policies be hugely motivating. The lump in the throat factor is rarely, if ever, there. I've never seen people read a policy and get emotional and inspired. I've never seen someone want to walk over hot coals to get to the other side for a policy. So why bother? Because they provide a mandate for action if and when people engage in counterproductive workplace behaviour or breach policy. As an example even the massively successful Wal-Mart retail giant has admitted the need for an about-face from high regulation of employee behaviour via policies to a shift to a values narrative. The company found that relying on policies alone to ensure staff compliance and good customer service has failed to have the desired impact on its workforce.

Many organisations may in fact be too big to include everyone in the development of the values. The staff involved therefore should consist of a genuinely representative sample from across the organisation. Regardless of whether it's a real-time strategic change event or a consultant-led series of focus groups and refinements, staff must feel as if they've had a chance to contribute. For extra clout, get the unions to sign off on them too.

The exercise we are talking about here by another name is 'a major cultural change initiative'. The former Harvard Business School professor and acclaimed leadership authority, John Kotter, has done excellent work in how to lead major culture change in an organisation. Reading his work in the area is highly recommended.

Strategy Step Two — Setting People Up to Win — The 'Pool Fence' Methodology

In the Australian State in which I live, it is compulsory to ensure adequate protection from the hazard of suburban pool drowning. Barriers in the form of gates and locks must safeguard against random access to backyard pools. Compliance with the legislation is achieved via a variety of methods including the installation of regulation-height fencing and childproof locks that make unauthorised access to the pool by small children difficult.

Likewise organisations must take a multifaceted approach to safeguard against behavioural transgressions such as harassment, sexual harassment, abuse of e-mail and the Internet, and bullying. A company may make all reasonable attempts to make it difficult for employees to transgress. If we take Internet use as the example, bars on certain websites, security software, firewalls, and access restrictions to certain levels or positions are all designed to make it hard for people to do the wrong thing. The pool equivalent is the side gate and lock, the high fence, and the childproof entry.

However, for any of us who've seen a small child clamber up the side of the fence and jump to the other side, there is no denying the fact that such obstructions are not foolproof. Inevitably, sensible parents may adopt the mentality that relying on the gates and fence height alone may not keep their children safe, so they teach their children to swim. They may also learn CPR so that in the unlikely event of a critical incident, they are ready with the appropriate emergency response.

And so it is with organisations: healthy and responsible organisations may adopt five complementary strategies to protect culture from wrongdoing, abuses, conflicts of interest, indiscretions, unethical practices including corruption, safety infringements, and life-threatening accidents.

The 'enlightened' organisation will:

1. Institute measures to minimise the chance of wrongdoing and the risk of reputational risk and other negative consequences (i.e., they will try to make it hard to do the wrong thing);

2. Educate people to make sensible and ethical decisions (i.e., they will try to make it easy and attractive to do the right thing);

3. Develop processes, policies, and protocols that enable a timely and coherent response in the event something bad happens;

4. Act on any transgressions proportionately and consistently;

5. Be proactive in setting the tone and tenor of a professional, respectful workplace so that doing the right thing and fostering a respectful, dynamic, healthy, and innovative workplace is as natural as breathing.

The only divergence in the analogy to the pool fencing is that in the event of accidental risk of drowning, all efforts would focus on saving the victim's life. The organisational response may need to focus initially on trying to determine the facts of the situation and the extent of any wrongdoing (thereby according the employee 'procedural fairness') but then centre on saving the culture or the team rather than the individual if the misconduct were found to justify disciplinary action or dismissal. Instead of saving the victim, the organisation may have to be willing to 'cut the tangled parachute' to save the life of the team and, indirectly, the organisation, although we don't jump to that as a first or even a second option. Unless the offending individual has been there all of five minutes, the organisation has enabled it. While it's easy to blame the individual, we will have more impact if we work on the organisation and resist the temptation to shoot the messenger!

Strategy Step Three — Embedding the Values Narrative as a Way of Life

Staff may be suspicious of the possibility that the introduction of a values narrative is nothing more than a fad. Some may decide that if they sit on their hands long enough, it will all go away. Therefore the values need to be incorporated into all training and reinforced at every turn, and senior leaders must coach employees about the values and the behaviours associated with them. Executives must view managers who are actively or passively working against them as high risk and decide whether they can afford to have those senior leaders stay on if they won't enlist.

In some cases, a strong push for a different way of being will result in some staff selecting out and voting with their feet. For those who hang around but won't play, the CEO may have to force their hand in either coming on board or getting off at the next station. With everyone watching, a gracious and respectful exit should be negotiated, as staff will take their cue from the leaders. It's not much good espousing respect as one of our values and then monstering someone on their way out of the organisation. The more staff know we are serious and committed, the more the dissenters are likely to decide to come on board or exit with their reputation and their references intact.

Supporting Strategies

Employee Selection — Starting with the Desired Culture in Mind

The American management consultant Peter Drucker said that culture eats strategy for breakfast. Similarly, good character supersedes any policy, no matter how well written.

Case Study — Indentifying Talent

Let me use an elite sports example. There is now an elaborate recruitment process within the Australian Football League (AFL) to identify talent from the early to mid teens. Young footballers with potential are scrutinised to within an inch of their lives by the time they are sixteen years old. Not only are they interviewed, pushed, and prodded, but so are their parents, their friends, and the friends of their friends. What clubs are trying to gauge beyond the footballer's aerobic capacity, technical prowess, fast twitch muscles and 'footy brain' mental toughness, is their strength of character. In a domain where demand for places at the highest level exceeds supply, the league can be choosy, and what it is choosing for when all the other boxes are ticked is character. In fact, some have gone so far as to say that character will sometimes be preferred over natural talent because if the fledgling players are made of the right stuff, they will withstand the extreme pressure and temptations and will be able to make the very best of the opportunities they are given.

In an era of social media, 24-hour news coverage, and a media appetite for scandal, AFL players must be motivated and able to protect their club's good name in their deeds and misdeeds. In an era where sponsors and players' parents are major gatekeepers to funding and player access respectively, good culture is paramount. That's one of the reasons player contracts are now choked with morals clauses. So mental toughness (i.e., emotional intelligence/resilience) and moral fibre both count.

The ultimate protection against counterproductive workplace behaviour then is to attempt to recruit people of good character and create a values narrative so they understand what the organisation stands for and what it will not tolerate. A holistic approach that drives values (and how to operationalise those values in everyday behaviour) is the path to success. The only issue, and it is a big one, is that existing organisations don't start from scratch.

So how do we test for character? Organisational psychologists can administer tests, and we can do behavioural interviewing that points in that direction, but realistically, companies may not be able to finance testing for people at all levels. Paying mind to character as an important attribute at the recruitment phase can assist. Every hire has the potential for delight or disaster in respect of culture. In an era where procedural fairness demands we accord employees every fair and reasonable chance to succeed and where performance management and termination of staff can be a protracted, tedious, and time-consuming process, it's better to proactively recruit for character than terminate for lack of it.

Accessing Personal Motivation and Fostering Engagement

It is logical that employees are less likely to bite the hand that feeds them (well). Engaged employees are more likely to want to come on board than those who are embittered, stale, or bruised. Counterproductive workplace behaviour happens in the context of poor moral norms of behaviour and absent, corrupt, or incompetent leadership, but it is also much more prevalent among disenfranchised staff.

Considering how much time employees spend at work, it is reasonable that they want more out of their work than just a pay cheque. I am however not going to extol here the virtues of meaningful work and how understanding the 'why' can drive the 'what' and the 'how'. Instead I would recommend you read the American management coach Dave Ulrich's excellent book, *The Meaning of Work* which showcases this issue beautifully.

However, if we help people enunciate what motivates them and help meet individual aspirations, staff may not have to act out to have their needs met. They are also less likely to want to pay out on the organisation because they are disaffected. Here, I would recommend the work of Dr. Ben Palmer, Australian psychologist, and founder of the Genos Organisation, who has conducted some fascinating and very contemporary research into ways to unlock employee performance by tapping into personal motivation as opposed to taking a one-size-fits-all approach to employee engagement.

A Compelling Vision (Or At Least Some Seriously Shared Goals)

As already stated, leaders and team members can enable *vulturesque* behaviour to be committed without negative consequences or challenge. But that is not to say that bad behaviour is always intentional. One of the fairest ways to head issues off at the pass is to eliminate the possibility that people just don't know. If people act out because they don't know what's right or wrong, we need to tell them and show them. We need to reward the behaviours we want to see more of. We need to call and invoke consequences for the behaviours we want to eliminate.

It's hard to get people to enlist in an unattractive cause. Some professional services firms ask me bewilderedly why morale is low and why so many of their good people leave. Inevitably, one of the partners is brave or angry enough to tell me what they're all really thinking. 'How dare they leave when we pay them so well!' In this case the firm lives under the flawed assumption that the staff should be *inspired* to make money to put into the partners' pockets. This is not likely to bring tears to the eyes or a lump to the throat unless you're a partner! Staff need a vision that's attractive and, if they are to stay motivated, it must also be attainable. There must be significance to the work they do. We take this for granted in the emergency department of a hospital, but for those of us not involved in the day-to-day drama of life-saving environments with lots of adrenalin, there must be some other meaning we can attach to what we do.

I am reminded here of work that was first done two decades ago by leadership experts Jim Kouzes and Barry Posner in their book *The Leadership Challenge*. They chronicled their research into how ordinary people can achieve extraordinary things. One of their case examples involved a university mailroom that had suffered from poor performance and low morale for a long time. When a new leader arrived and actively intervened, outputs and customer service soared. What was the difference? The leader helped the mailroom personnel redefine their vision, which took them from 'We're just a mailroom' to 'We keep the whole university connected'. This is finding an attractive way to sell the 'why' of what we do rather than fixate on 'what has to be done, by when, and by whom'. If lofty vision isn't your thing, the very least we need to establish is shared goals.

Performance Management — A Broader Definition

Who typically tends to get the most attention in organisations? Most of us would agree it's either the problem children or the stars. We can neglect the others at the centre of the bell curve who just come to work each day to do their jobs. The best organisations actively performance manage all staff. That is, they create a feedback culture where performance dialogue spans the year, and people have a good sense of the contributions they make and how they can improve. It is imperative that performance management is not (just) the stuff we do when someone is in trouble. We limit the scope and potential of performance management when it becomes known as a reactive process that 'could result in disciplinary action up to and including dismissal'.

Performance management needs to embrace the whole spectrum of positive and sustained performance and behaviour through to what is toxic, dysfunctional, and unacceptable. And yes, at times, it may also involve taking strong action.

One quick and decisive way to shift culture is to remove a critical mass of people believed to stand for the 'wrong' things. It's the workplace version of cutting out the cancer. It's efficient but not always respectful, and it can be a reputational nightmare. It can create gross insecurity in other staff, who may wonder whether they will be next. If we want to model respectful, ethical behaviour, than slashing and burning sends a mixed message. It's like the parent who hits a child because the child is being violent to a sibling. Remember that we get what we deserve.

The pool fence analogy described earlier also works on the principle of educate first, shift mindset, grow skills, and only 'punish' as a last resort. Many years ago, I attended a work-sponsored seminar with a performance management guru at an inner city hotel. We were all there to establish the answer to one question, 'Why is it that some employees don't do what you want them to do?' Finally, the guru came to that answer. We all held our breath, pens poised for what would be illuminating and earth shattering. I was expecting the ground to move beneath my feet. His answer to the question was as follows:

- They don't know what to do, *or*
- They don't know how to do it, *or*
- They just don't wanna!

Well, we were a little underwhelmed, and I dare say some people wanted their money back. However, all these years later, I have more appreciation for his pearls of wisdom. Work on the *will* and give people the *skill* before labelling them as lazy or obstructive.

The implications are that when using performance management we need to devise the context, values, and behaviours we want our people to adopt, create a compelling '*why*' this matters and then the *how* to live to those frameworks, support them actively and genuinely in transitioning to that new way of 'being', then measure and reward the extent to which they live such values.

Case Study — Values in Action, Pool Fence, and Policies

I have a current client who is doing the culture-change piece superbly, but it has been a long, hard road of meetings with staff, unions, and consultants to get there. The company introduced a code of conduct last year and has moved this year to the ratification of a behavioural capability framework that it wants to use as an aspirational tool to grow people around culture and performance. The code of conduct is regarded as the bare minimum acceptable standard of behaviour. The behavioural capability framework goes beyond that to the sorts of behaviours designed to bring about high performance in mindset and in actuality. Things like connectedness, innovation, and emotional resilience are what the company is now striving for to sit above expectations of respect for the individual, zero tolerance of harassment and bullying, and avoidance of conflicts of interest.

Over the coming year, the company is also moving to integrate the desired behaviours into criteria for advancement so that people will come to understand that this stuff isn't a 'nice to have' but is the basis for advancement in the organisation in harmony with the technical and leadership capabilities required in senior roles. The ultimate proof of its success will be the elevation of people in the organisation who manifest the best of interpersonal skills, leadership, and emotionally intelligent behaviour coupled with research or educational prowess and desire to grow others around them. The company's fervent hope is people won't any longer experience the cynicism and disenchantment of highly intelligent loners, or bullies being elevated above those with team orientation and emotional intelligence. The organisation is not saying the qualities that were important before have ceased to matter. What it has done is expand the range of attributes seen as business critical and will recruit, select, train, coach, and ultimately reward the combination. The other symbolic premise of this methodology is that it no longer elevates technical and scientific staff over the professional managerial staff. The behaviours are seen to be critical across both populations and reinforce what unites the two populations of staff far more than what previously divided them (e.g. formal qualifications).

An intensive rollout of briefings, training sessions, and a communication strategy are working in harmony to increase the will and the skill to deliver the capability framework. The first few weeks of the training rollout have been very promising. Senior staff, many of whom have been in the organisation a long time, are excited because they see it as the missing link in what they've tried to do without the official organisational mandate they have now.

Thus awareness raising, mindset shifting, and skills training must be bolted on to the actual framework itself. These elements are the water safety education, swimming lessons, and CPR training to accompany the construction of the pool fence.

We thus have cause to be optimistic about what can be done to turn around organisations where there is a compelling need to do so and we've deployed enough people with enough influence to make it happen. One thing we can rely on consistently is for people to act in their own best interests. I am not being cynical in saying that, nor is it necessarily a weakness. We would not have survived as a species if we did not have an innate predisposition to self-preservation. Having said that, we can also harness the altruistic desires in people by helping them see that if they build a good culture, they are doing something great for everyone except those who want to pull it down.

It's important to remember you don't have to bring everyone with you to achieve a 'tipping point'. You do however have to send a clear message that the context has changed and that your people need to change with it; that there is a need to create a compelling and preferably inspiring picture of what 'good' looks like and why it matters. You have to ensure people get the fact that you are 100 percent committed to changing things and that you have the courage and the determination to do so. You do have to tighten processes, act on indiscretions (after you've warned and educated), and enlist champions to help you get there. And you do have to empower people to make a choice about whether they want to come along for the ride and commit to coming, not just to sitting on the train with you every day as a reluctant passenger and then write to the ombudsman in complaint.

In the previous chapter, we talked about the critical success factors to achieving organisational change. But we have to have a methodology too. Before people will move, we have to shock them out of their complacency, denial, or justifications. This can only happen if we successfully make the point that the context has changed and what we're doing is not working. In other words, harness the will, and then develop the skill.

Creating the Imperative for Change — The Culture Audit

A culture audit, health and well-being assessment, and organisational review (psychosocial not structural) are all variations on the same thing. Some consulting firms have outstanding engagement surveys and quantitative climate surveys. They churn out results, but the organisation has to have the stomach to hear the messages its staff are trying to share. I wish I had a dollar for every time I was invited to meet a prospective new client who told me about the elaborate and expensive explorations it performed with outside help from prestigious firms only to put the findings in a drawer or on a shelf, never to be seen again. I can only deduce in these situations:

- They couldn't make sense of what the results told them,
- They refused to accept the veracity of the survey results,
- They didn't have the stomach to do anything (because perhaps it was too overwhelming), or
- The consultants failed to help them devise ways of going about it.

Before an organisation commissions an audit, it is critical to come to a shared agreement with the executive leadership on what to do with the findings. My preference is for qualitative research. I am less interested in what proportion of staff feels safe to raise issues of concern in the workplace and more concerned about why those who can't, don't! Then again, if 60 percent feel that way, that's enough of a reason to put on the SWAT team hat and 'go in'. The open comments fields in such instruments are invaluable, but I have always found there were questions I wanted to ask after reading through the results but no one was in the room to answer me. Of course, in an online survey, there is no group dynamic weighing in on the individual survey response that can contaminate the results. Grandstanding or groupthink in the focus group can play havoc with your heart-felt desire to get to the truth, but if well facilitated, one normally extracts enough invaluable information to serve as a jumping-off point into analysis and tentative formulation of strategies to shift them.

Of course sometimes a culture is so bad that you might as well save your money on the audit and just focus your energy on determining whether it can be saved.

Case Study — Work Insurance Woes

A few years ago, I was approached by an HR executive to conduct an investigation into a bullying complaint at a subur-ban food plant. The bullying complaint had emanated from a work insurance matter. I was not surprised to learn that a stress claim might have arisen from alleged bullying. I was far more surprised to learn that the claimant had allegedly been bullied by the work insurance manager handling his claim. This was the matter I was to investigate. My first meeting when I came onsite was with the HR Manager who told me a tale of woe about the organisation's culture. The present owners had pur-chased the company from a third-generation family business some two years before but had not expected the degree of dysfunction, hostility, sense of entitlement, and 'corruption' they encountered.

I recall vividly what she told me:

'You need to understand, Leanne, that no one actually resigns from this place. The vast majority of staff go off on stress, never to return, or are given lucrative redundancy packages as they get older and can no longer meet the inherent requirements of the job. The majority of people still here are biding time in the hope they get offered a package too. In fact, some of them play up badly in the hope we'll decide to package them out. And currently, 30 percent of our workforce are off on stress'.

She was obviously nervous to have shared information with me; her eyes darted furtively around the room as if she were being watched or recorded. When I asked her whether there was any chance we could do some work together to try to turn things around, she said she had to fight for the chance to bring in an external investigator as the company was very keen to suppress any public perception the place was entirely hostile and dysfunctional (there were rumours floating around about an intention to sell).

My job was to determine on the balance of probabilities whether the female work insurance manager had bullied the claimant in the course of administering his claim. The claimant alleged the manager withheld payment unreasonably, forced him to comply with onerous paperwork demands, and was otherwise trying to intimidate him back to work.

The manager had been in her role for just under twelve months. She came into the organisation knowing the insurance cover situation was totally out of hand and was given a mandate to actively manage cases to the letter of the law. She was told not to unreasonably obstruct any of the employees but to ensure people complied with timelines and paperwork completion, all of which was stipulated by the insurance company.

The claimant had alleged he slipped on some stairs and jarred his knee. He had an arthroscopy, which would normally have left someone stiff and sore for around ten days. Three months later, he was still limping and on crutches. His doctor said he was not permitted to do virtually every job on site except one low-impact set of tasks that had to be performed on day shift, yet the claimant alleged he had been bullied by the work insurance manager and wanted to work afternoons so he could take his young daughter to school every day. The manager said she had consulted with management and that there were no other roles he could perform based on the restrictions set out by his doctor, save the one on day shift. The injured worker said this was a conspiracy to get him back to work to reinjure himself. Yet, he also broke down and told me he was still at home 'recovering', missing his friends acutely, and suffering through his wife's bitter complaints that their whole lives had been disrupted.

I interviewed the claimant, the work insurance manager, and, at the claimant's insistence, the head union delegate. His office was an air-conditioned on-site caravan, and he asked me to interview him there. When I met with him, a large, tall, and aggressive man, he made it clear the claimant was being treated appallingly and that he had instructed him not to come to work at all until the company accommodated his wishes. When I suggested the claimant did not appear to be coping that well at home, he said tersely that this was not for me to say and that he would continue to guide the claimant on the best way forward. He stood over me at the end of our interview and insisted I hand over my rough written notes, which I politely declined to do. I said I would be more than happy for him to review and sign my typed copy of his statement.

After meeting with other potential witnesses, I determined there was insufficient evidence to conclude the work insurance manager had bullied the claimant. Her worst crime appeared to have been refusing to reimburse medical expenses until he had completed and signed the required paperwork. She was relieved to learn the complaint was unsubstantiated, but I was not surprised to learn she left the company some three months later and took six months off work for burnout. Off the record, I can tell you I deduced she was being bullied by the claimant and the union delegate and was inadequately supported by the organisation that sent her into a war zone with no backup and unarmed.

Ultimately, the organisation dealt with the issue of toxic culture it obviously felt was unsalvageable by selling off that division. All staff were made redundant. The buyer didn't want any of them. Sadly, there was every likelihood that many of them would not find subsequent employment. Thus, the strong action taken effectively ended their careers.

This was a very extreme case of unchecked culture that was allowed to implode. Depending on the current state of culture, intervening at the level of the organisation is sound but time and resource consuming. Sometimes it's not necessary to work with the whole organisation. It can just be one team or department that needs fixing. The next chapter provides a methodology for how to do that.

Chapter 11

Strategies for Culture Change at the Team Level

t its most basic, any work team is a microcosmic organisation; thus, what we have recommended needs to be put in place for a team reflects the imperatives for the bigger organisation. We advocate the combination of creating a values narrative, choosing staff preciously, imbuing team members with an understanding of why we exist and why that matters, and demonstrating leadership in enacting values every day. We need to help staff by modelling the values in visible behaviour, practising them, affirming them, rewarding and recognising them, and calling and 'consequencing' any deviation from them.

As for the critical success factors in shifting a team, all of the same factors apply as before, with a couple of additions. For it to work, team leaders need to have real motivation, muster up courage, make time, practise patience, and be prepared to act on deviance from shared behaviours. They also need to ensure they strike a healthy balance with all members of the team, as enmeshment (too close to be objective in work relationships) and detachment (too removed to know what is going on or too 'hands off' to 'call' it) may be some of the features of a team environment that allowed toxic or unlawful behaviour to flourish.

Striking a Professional Relationship Balance

Specifically, for teams to thrive, we have found that managers and team leaders need to strike a healthy cultural balance in a pleasant, yet businesslike relationship with their people. Yes, there are definitely some employees who have a love affair with their companies. Many Apple and Google employees would be examples, but I don't think their employees necessarily think they are immunised against accountability. Employers can and should be loyal to employees in times of crisis, but good organisations don't let the ship go down with the passenger.

So demonstrated care, in contrast to *detachment*, is vitally important. But at the other extreme, *enmeshment* is not healthy either. It compromises the professional distance and objectivity that make courageous conversations and disciplinary action possible.

Critical Success Factors for Culture Change at the Team Level

The factors already identified as critical to a company's change success apply to a work team. Someone has to drive the change, be committed to overcoming resistance, be candid and self-aware as to how things got to where they did, and be willing to take responsibility for turning things around. But the responsible person may need to draw on the big guns to make that happen, so he or she may need to deploy added authority. And, this person may face a team of people who are vested in keeping things as they are or who are low on confidence in their ability to make the change and have that change stick.

The Impact of a New Leader

I have seen great movement in a team with the arrival of a new leader who signals very swiftly, articulately, and maybe even inspiringly that he or she stands for a particular set of values and won't tolerate certain 'below the line' behaviours. The signalling that the leader won't allow certain behaviours to be committed and willingness to call them at the first sign of them surfacing can send a strong and powerful message to the rest of the troops that echoes, in the immortal words of Tevye in *Fiddler on the Roof*, 'It's a new veldt (world), Golde!'

Of course, the leader who first calls something that hitherto flew under the radar has to maintain vigilance, be consistent, and not play politics about who gets a serve and who doesn't. The leader will quickly lose respect if a poor performing employee gets grief for abusive or harassing behaviour but the equally guilty top salesperson doesn't. People will see through that and lose heart and respect quickly. I can hear them now:

> *I was so hopeful when the new leader arrived. I thought this person had real integrity, but now I see there are different rules for different people. That much hasn't changed. I really started to believe, but now I'm even more disillusioned. The old leader played favourites in deciding who got to play golf with him on the weekend. The new leader plays favourites about who can behave badly and who can't.*

Despite this, we do know that one person can make a big difference. Dramatic things can happen as someone enters a team and as someone departs. I recall an operations manager in manufacturing telling me about the appointment of the company's first female engineer on a major infrastructure project. He talked candidly of his anxiety in bringing her into such a macho 'blokey' environment, where even the most robust and resilient would sometimes go weak at the knees. He was strong in his belief that he should not 'play dad', as he called it, and deny her the opportunity in order to protect her, as she was well qualified. He was also of the belief that diversity in a team is normal and healthy, and maintaining the status quo would, by definition, never bring about a change in culture. He was confident he had prepared her for what she was walking into, and that she was up for the challenge. He also made it clear to her that he was there for support and she must not hesitate to come to him if she found it tough going or if the team attempted to sabotage her success. Some months later, he told me he was delighted. The introduction of mixed gender to that rugged environment had brought about some positive changes. The guys, by their own admission, had cleaned up their act, and she reported them as being extremely respectful and protective of her if they came up against contractors or suppliers who attempted to give them a hard time for 'selling out to political correctness'.

Now I acknowledge that she was excellent at her work, and their respect for her was entirely appropriate and deserved. She could have viewed their protective tendencies as disempowering. The fact is, she didn't, and it worked for that group. The inclusion of one person made a positive difference.

Conversely, the inclusion of one person can totally shake a team to its foundations in the worst possible way. Some teams become depressed as they contemplate the end of their world as they knew it. Some find themselves being led by an incompetent person and succeed *despite* the leader. The leader can become even more unpopular if seen to be taking the credit for what he or she inherited.

If the disruptive person is the new team leader, we can understand how one person can have a negative impact. The leader role is usually a powerful one. However, one person joining a team as an equal participant can still wield considerable disruptive power in context.

We will deal with the disruptive or toxic leader as a threat to good culture in the next chapter. But for now, let's outline a powerful methodology for getting teams (including departments or divisions) back on track.

Methodology for Culture Change in a Team

Step One — Onboarding

We need to herald the decision for change and introduce and talk up those who will lead it. Those first few messages, meetings, and introductions are critical to create positive expectancy at best and curiosity at worst. You may want to use an experienced consultant to assist with the change and the associated communication, but the internal team must be integrally involved and visible.

Step Two — Provide Incontrovertible Proof That Our Current Way of Being Is Not Working

This can be done with some metrics, but if there is considerable mistrust, it is better to conduct a qualitative survey with individual and small groups and report the findings. Thus, we have our burning platform as one of our two major drivers for change.

It may also become apparent in this qualitative culture audit (emphasis on what's not working) or health and well-being assessment (emphasis on safety and well-being) that particular relationships have broken down and must be addressed for the team to have some hope of success. The other things to look for here are whether the leadership team itself is cohesive or fractured and whether the leader is credible, courageous, and authoritative (or not), as we may need to embark on some precursor or concurrent remedial strategies to minimise risk and maximise the chances of success.

Step Three — Synthesise and Report Back

Synthesise (de-identified, of course) the major themes in the intelligence that has been gathered and share the results (prior to or at an event). Then ask the team whether it is prepared to do what it takes to make a change. I will always ask people for comments and their opinion on whether what I've shared is a true and accurate reflection of the real state of affairs. It is very powerful for them to sit there in heavy silence or to nod heads or verbalise that we have 'got it right' on the current state of play, particularly when we have presented unflattering portrayals or a downright destructive picture. They recognise they can do better and they have the right to want better. The organisation must then deliver on a way to get there without blame or humiliation.

Step Four — Align with the Company Values Narrative or Prepare to Create Team Values and Behaviours

If the organisation has an existing framework, then the team can develop its own set of values and behaviours that align with those of the organisation or work on how it might adopt and live the same organisational values in what it does every day in dealing with each other, clients, and suppliers. The alignment needs to be incorporated in the communications strategy about the culture change. The actual generation of values and associated behaviours needs to be done or at least begun at the event (see below).

What is exciting and daunting about working at the team level is that the team is often small enough to be more easily accessible, and interventions can be done with everyone in real time. We can see significant shifts almost overnight, provided that people are committed. However, the relationships are intense with day-to-day contact, and one or two people who don't want to come along for the ride can make it hard for the rest to take an unfettered run at the prize.

There can also be some guilt and discomfort in embracing the need for change when close colleagues are railing against any change, so the dynamics in these relationships need to be managed carefully. It can also happen that the vast majority of the team wants to move but one or two don't, and they are — no surprise — some of the most influential and stand to lose the most by any change in terms of power base. However, the power of the team can be significant. Even one strong person taking one end of the rope in a tug of war can be pulled across by several on the other side pulling in unison in the other direction.

Step Five — Real Time Culture Change (An Intervention Event or Series of Events)

I advocate conducting an event or a series of small workshops to get people on board whilst being careful to manage the individual self-esteem and allow them to save face. It is critical to incorporate pre- and post-work. Run the event that allows the organisation to operationalise the values in action and call for commitment to a way forward. Spend time and effort working to create a mindset for success. In pre-event communication, I ask people to bring a sense of adventure and an open mind.

At the event, I ask them to brainstorm those things that *could* make the organisation fail (with the clear implication we are not going to allow that to happen!) and those things that *will* help the organisation succeed. Warn them that relationships require compromise, possibly even forgiveness, and the choice to let go of prior baggage. But do not be esoteric about that. Be emotionally honest with them and explain they may have to give up some of their most cherished beliefs. They may have to let go of anger, resentment, and bitterness and take a leap of faith, that is, take risks without a guarantee someone else will do the same.

For those who can't or won't go along with the plan, the organisation must develop an out for them or, if they won't go voluntarily, an out for the organisation (see chapter 12 — Strategies for Culture Change at the Individual Level).

Step Six — Follow Up and Embed

Continue to work with those who are seriously damaged. They may need to access the Employee Assistance Program or be offered emotional intelligence/resilience/conflict coaching, etc. Depending on their background and experience, sometimes the consultant assisting with the change is perfectly placed to work with them in the aftermath of an event because they have shared the journey, understand the issues, met the people, and can encourage optimism and continue to coach for resilience.

Continue to work with those who need assistance to conform to the new ways of behaving, as some will have been active contributors to any prior dysfunction (i.e., set people up to win). Keep working with the leadership and provide support so they hold their nerve when a few staunch resisters dig their heels in or act out as the system becomes unstable.

Case Study — Team Methodology in Action

A university approached me about toxic behaviour that was occurring in one of its schools. The school had seen three acting heads of school come and go in three years and felt quite unloved and professionally embarrassed. This didn't seem to curtail the bad behaviour at all as routinely people sent each other vitriolic e-mails, indulged in game playing, point scoring, naming and shaming at meetings, aggression and intimidation — all of which served to undermine the university's reputation with stakeholders outside the school and contributed to missed deadlines, lots of stress, and absenteeism.

A new manager had been appointed, and while people generally regarded her as highly credible and likeable, she was besieged in her first few weeks with people queuing up outside her door to share tales of woe — about everyone else. Upon hearing of her appointment, three people in her industry sector told her she was making a mistake to go there, as the school's reputation had spread far and wide. The school had been advised it would lose its vocational accreditation with an outside body if it didn't get its act together, rewrite some curricula, and improve student outcomes.

When I met the new manager, she was haggard and overwrought. She was second-guessing the decision she had made to take the role and rued walking away from a great job. She told me confidentially that she had been asked to go back to her old place of employ and she was considering it, even though she went to pains to tell me she was not normally a quitter. She said the rivalry between the staff on two different floors was so bad that each faction seemed to get jealous and hostile when she had lunch with the other team (in a bid to get to know them), so she had taken to eating her lunch in her office every day. She acknowledged she had ostensibly cut herself off, which also meant she was not in a position to positively change the culture.

I asked her what would need to happen for her to feel she wanted to stay. I coached her around fighting her instinct to withdraw. We agreed she would get out there and be even-handed but connected. She would assume the best in everyone but call the worst every time she saw it. We agreed that I would embark on a qualitative staff survey using confidential interviews and teleconferences, and she would fight for budget for an event.

She explained that one of the worst offenders had been counselled for an outrageous e-mail and was currently on stress leave. We both regarded that decision as a protest. However, on balance, we thought we might be able to do some good work with the team if he wasn't there. We agreed she would advise him of our upcoming workshop and give him the choice to attend but live with either decision and not put him under undue pressure. He declined to be interviewed as part of my data-gathering exercise or to attend the team workshop, so we knew we needed to put something in place to fill him in when he returned on what he missed.

I followed the model outlined in this chapter. Those who attended were quite anxious at the start of the day, but I applauded them for investing enough to show up. It was important for them to know I had worked extensively in their sector and that I was not there to judge or embarrass them. We worked our way through the themed interviews presentation, and there were some tears. However, they were all prepared to acknowledge the situation was as dire as people had portrayed it individually and that they all deserved and wanted better.

We spent the major part of the day working on a behaviour charter and agreed they would get some e-mail training to manage tone and tenor as well as volume. Two staff – one previously quite negative in outlook who warmed up during the day and another more moderate – agreed to brief the absent staff member on the day's proceedings. The senior manager was sufficiently hopeful by the end of that day to stay on.

Since the intervention, she has had to counsel the errant staff member, who returned to the workplace one more time. In all probability, she will end up dismissing him if he transgresses on behavioural grounds again. Even those who were his previous allies have distanced themselves, as they find the workplace so much more pleasant now. I continue to coach the senior manager about embedding the change. We have now turned our minds to better role clarity and interdependencies between staff to upgrade the quality of what they do now that they can work together more constructively. She remains happy she stayed on and so is the team, as they now have a supportive and savvy leader who is committed to excellence and to them.

Case Study — Team Methodology in Action Post-Grievance

I use this case because many themes we have discussed throughout the book are in play here.

I was approached to conduct a bullying investigation in a government department. Some of the same protagonists to be interviewed had been interviewed for a previous investigation some three years before. The original complaint had named the senior manager as the respondent, although the claim had been unsubstantiated. This complaint implicated her direct report.

The two came originally from the same organisation, with the senior manager arriving here first. Some staff had suspicions about how their manager came to get the job with the current organisation and harboured some bitterness because they said they never had the chance to apply. Folklore held that the two managers had been extremely close and had instituted some significant changes in their previous department, something which had been regarded as well executed and entirely legitimate. Staff here were anxious about mooted changes and were allegedly intimidated by aggressive treatment from their manager, which they said always seemed to be supported or justified by the senior manager, and they felt quite unsafe. One person filed a complaint, but it became clear when interviewing other witnesses that if they had not been so scared of victimisation, several others may have been prompted to lodge a grievance.

The bigger context of the grievance was significant change in the department's business, including the ongoing threat of outsourcing. The managers had continued to reassure their people there was no intent to outsource their work, but trust was very low. Staff were almost paranoid and quite traumatised by bad treatment and isolation. What seemed to add to their stress and insecurity was that the immediate manager was not very competent, took credit for some of their work, and appeared to have been overzealous in his attempts to improve efficiency amongst already dedicated but overloaded staff. The staff had a lot of respect for the senior manager's ability but felt hamstrung by the relationship between the senior manager and their own manager. They said they felt they were out on their own.

It was true that the senior manager was generally highly thought of in the business for her technical ability, but fair to say, not for her interpersonal skills.

A number of things conspired against team members' sense of security in the system. The spectre of change as well as high-level support for the senior manager from the CEO down helped create a feeling of invincibility in the senior manager and her direct report. By all accounts, the team manager had fits of rage, made unreasonable demands, sent hostile e-mails, and generally undermined the staff.

I remain convinced that many of the changes the two managers were trying to institute were perfectly sound and reasonable. Were the emotional climate different in the team, the team members may have been able to embrace them more readily.

However, stylistically, the manager was impatient, aggressive, and overly protected – even enabled – by the senior manager, who had a clear mandate to institute major change and seemed content to let her one-down manager kick heads to get things moving.

I substantiated the claim of bullying. The organisation decided not to dismiss but placed the respondent on final warning. It explained that any further violations of the company's values or behaviour of a similar nature would threaten his employment. The organisation elected to transfer the respondent to another branch for the sake of the health and safety of his team. He took up a position as a senior analyst with no direct reports on a project that could make good use of his skills.

In the grievance debrief, he was initially very angry and resentful in being told he would be moving until he was reminded that many such informal complaints had been made about him over a period of some years, that the whole team was stressed and that this could not be ignored. The CEO and I agreed we would not disclose the fact that the investigation process revealed a number of other potential complaints waiting to happen to minimise the risk of victimisation. He was offered short-term behavioural coaching, which he took up to help him understand what did and didn't constitute bullying. In the few sessions with him, I observed his anger dissipating. Over time, he came to understand the transfer represented a fresh start for him as part of a new team.

In addition, we debriefed the outworkings of the case with the senior manager with the CEO in attendance to add gravitas to the findings and next steps. We pointed out a few inconsistencies in her testimony and explained it was critical for the long-term success of her team that she came on board with the organisa-tion's values. Without identifying any witnesses, we talked about staff insecurity and the mistrust they had, due mostly to the per-ceived close friendship between the two parties. The CEO put it quite directly and skilfully to the senior manager that her loyalty had to lie with the organisation first and foremost and that she had a team of very stressed and intimidated employees for which the senior manager had to take ultimate responsibility. The senior manager was very honest in her annoyance that her one-down manager was being transferred, as she saw them as being in sync with each other on where they wanted to take the branch. The CEO assertively differentiated the legitimacy of the change mandate with the importance of ensuring that management didn't lose its way in justifying any improper means to achieve the ends.

I have done many investigations where I am there to come to a determination, make some recommendations, and leave. Indeed, this is almost always what full-time investigators and lawyers do when tasked with the same job. The difference in being an organisational psychologist and a systems thinker is in being able to conceptualise the number of factors that may have been at play and to work multiple interventions and variables in bringing the team to a stable place once again. In this case study whilst I determined the manager had bullied, to patholo- gise one person in this situation would be to negate the other factors that contributed to, and exacerbated, the situation to the detriment of all team members. To focus all our energy on whether anything unlawful occurred would be to ignore the other factors that contributed to poor health and well-being and that needed to be addressed for staff members to heal.

Yes, I ran an investigation, which on the face of it seemingly pointed at one bully. However, we then intervened with the senior manager, assisted in the recruitment of a new manager with all the right qualities (including character), recommended another consultant to do some team development with the new team post-grievance (as I thought it was important to separate the disciplinary process from the aspirational process), and I provided psychological support to a few individuals who needed to do some healing over the first few months post-grievance.

There are many examples of vulturesque behaviour that are sometimes little more than a reflection of clumsy execution of good ideas or decisive leadership. That is, the individual or the team is genuinely motivated to do the right thing. A lack of nous, empathy, diplomacy or skill gets in the way. The individual or team pushes too hard for results, misunderstands the way change is to be implemented, and confuses and micromanages. And of course, not all examples of wrongdoing can come down to misguided incompetence. Sometimes an individual team member is a disaster waiting to happen when placed in a system that enables the worst of what he or she has to offer.

The next chapter outlines some of the characters typically found to be most difficult along with some strategies designed to shift them or, in the worst-case scenario, ship them out.

Chapter 12

Strategies for Culture Change at the Individual Level
(Organisational Response to the Lone Vulture)

'It's amazing. You can't believe how badly you got it wrong. And then you go back to the psychometric testing in the personnel file and the concerns that were identified or the markers that should have given you 'cause for pause' and you think, 'why oh why did we hire this person?'

Why didn't we listen to the recruitment consultant, the referee, or our own gut feelings? Plenty of reasons. Maybe the recruitment consultant didn't highlight any of the negatives. She wanted to make the placement. The referee may have seen it as an opportunity to get rid of a problem child and was all too happy to provide a good reference or a veiled one. He may have declined to give a reference at all if it was against company policy. And as for your gut? Your gut also told you it's unfair to judge people you hardly know. Or you mused, 'Once this person gets into our environment, they'll be fine'. Or 'Perhaps they only stayed where they were a short time because the organisation there was toxic'. Or 'I'm just so tired from being chronically short-staffed and no one is going to be perfect', so near enough is good enough. Except it wasn't.

The Responsibility

The organisation has the responsibility to create and maintain a healthy system, but what should it do with the individual? The responsibility is a dual one; for the individual as a continuing member of staff *and* for the organisation, which must not be terrorised by a bad hire or someone who has imploded under pressure. Clearly, in the first instance, if the organisation decides the person should stay or there are insufficient grounds to remove the person, it must be clear, consistent, and resolute about the need for the person to conform to the company's values and agreed behaviours and that noncompliance cannot be tolerated. Of course, it is critical here to determine whether the person has failed to do so because he or she doesn't have the *will* or the *skill* or both. We can be more tolerant of those who need to develop skills than those whose lack of empathy for others and unprofessional conduct knows no bounds.

If it's the will, the person needs to know his or her job is in jeopardy if he or she continues to flout the values and behaviours of the organisation (or the team).

If it's a case of wanting to do the right thing but not knowing how, coaching, awareness training (e.g., ethics training), or interpersonal skills training may help.

The second part of our responsibility beyond wanting to ensure people do not 're-offend' is to continue to show demonstrated care for employees and to optimise their performance as well as their conduct. I have included a short section on parallel processes in recognition of the fact that discovering some *vulturesqueness* is occurring or concluding an investigation and sharing the news can't be the end of it for the victim/complainant, the offender/respondent, and often the team/system.

Interventions

Coaching

Coaching can be a great option for one-on-one time with coachees that can accelerate their development, including their emotional intelligence. But only if the coachees are *motivated*. In my experience, it doesn't really matter if they are motivated because they wish to be nominated for sainthood down the track or because they are scared of losing their job under serious misconduct provisions in a company policy. I can work with either. However, coaching is not a magic bullet solution, particularly if the coachees don't want what you're selling or will revel in the attention of the opportunity to bag the organisation or continue to shirk any self-responsibility.

Case Study — Shutting the Gate after the Horse Has Bolted

This manager was a nightmare. He swore, he yelled, he threw tantrums at the drop of a hat. People would come into work some days shaking and quaking, and would have a code that rated his mood so people would know whether it was safe to go into his office. No one in upper management seemed to care because he was a schmoozer and had great relationships with the external clients. He was a gambler and a boozer and took clients to the corporate box at the cricket, which they loved. They rewarded him with a lot of business, and staff could never understand why no one outside the company saw through him.

One by one, all the talented people left. After they had lost about eight good people and senior management woke up to the fact that this guy was destructive, the organisation offered him coaching. The rest of the staff knew things weren't going to change, and the sense of hopelessness got worse, except now people didn't just think senior management was ignorant, they thought they were gutless too.

Critical Incident and Investigation Debriefing

As opposed to long-term coaching, as a bare minimum, it is vital that there is a debriefing session with offenders/respondents and victims/targets/complainants after determinations are made about what to do with the offending individual (whether internally or by an external jurisdiction).

Victims/targets/complainants need to understand the findings (without sharing the confidential specifics of the organisation's response against the perpetrator). They need a chance to express their reaction, see demonstrated care by leadership, be offered additional support to heal, and have an opportunity to ask any questions on issues that may concern them. This could include wanting to know what others have been told about the grievance or rupture in the relationship, how others understand any absence they may have taken, and how much of the circumstances or their own feelings, if anything, can be shared. They may fear victimisation if the respondent was popular or had attempted to garner support in the early stages of the grievance before there was a 'gag order' on both parties talking about it with people at work.

If one dramatic incident precipitated a complaint (or a strong organisational response), the complainant could be traumatised and hypervigilant to future behaviour from the respondent. The hardest thing to do is to restore comfort for both parties in the immediate aftermath of a serious complaint, as victims/targets/complainants are typically scared of retaliation, peer rejection, or further occurrences of the offensive behaviour, and the offenders/respondents are inevitably fearful of retaliation, peer rejection, and further allegations of wrongdoing that could threaten their employment. It is unfortunate yet fascinating to observe respondents after they have been found to have intimidated or threatened others, become so fearful that the recipient of their unwelcome attention might be now trying to set them up, with the resultant reciprocal fear.

Respondents need what I refer to as the 'Do they get it?' interview. Many of my clients understand the importance of letting respondents process their reaction, ask questions, and determine how they can re-enter the workplace if there has been a period of voluntary or forced absence. They may still be angry and harbour significant resentment toward the complainant and/or the organisation. These should be addressed by an experienced debriefer, organisational psychologist, or highly skilled senior manager. There needs to be some sort of expert assessment as to what needs to be done to help respondents (assuming they get to keep their job) re-enter the workplace smoothly post-determination. Similarly, as part of this, there needs to be some sort of risk assessment that the respondent could victimise the complainant once back in the workplace.

The policy and legislation around victimisation should be emphasised with both complainant and respondent, as both should be able to move on constructively post-grievance once any disciplinary action is meted out without punishing the respondent over and over again. If the respondent is remorseful, keen to grow, and wants to stay out of trouble, the first 'Do they get it?' interview can also be the opportunity to set some behavioural outcomes for a series of productive coaching sessions.

In many cases, the respondent decides the best way to keep out of trouble is to refuse to deal with the complainant at all. This may well suit the complainant, but if they stay on the same team and you can cut the air with a knife during meetings, there will have to be some elegant intervention. In my experience clients that have handled this best have usually created some short-term buffer zone between the parties but made it clear this will not be a permanent arrangement. Sometimes the respondent doesn't want the continual pressure and starts looking for another job externally, which, in some cases, is not a bad thing for anyone. Often complainants, team members, management, and HR are relieved and delighted when someone who did something not quite bad enough to constitute a dismissible offence sees the writing on the wall and decides to go flourish elsewhere.

Interpersonal Skills Training

While training is an obvious way forward it must be remembered that it is far easier to provide professional development for motivated learners. My observation is that those organisations that demand respondents attend a one-off awareness session are doing so as a tokenistic gesture that ticks the box for compliance purposes. Expecting that people who may have engaged in pervasive, systematic, or multiple occurrences of offensive behaviour are going to be 'cured' in the space of one briefing is naïve.

Even if they are motivated, they may need a lot of support to be able to shift from displaying bullying tendencies to becoming a supportive manager. Even so, a training course, followed up by active support from their one-up manager, may work well if they agree on the outcomes to be achieved in the training ahead of time and work diligently afterwards to continue to apply the learnings.

If the behavioural issues of concern involve the respondents' inability to control their emotions under pressure and they need emotional intelligence training or coaching, it is important that the organisation be realistic and fair in expecting this will take many weeks and even months to achieve. Whatever the respondents were doing up until the point at which they got into trouble, they have probably been behaving that way for years, if not decades. Developing self-awareness and emotional control can be a lengthy journey, if not a lifelong one, for people who've developed deeply ingrained patterns of behaviour that to some significant degree must have served them well (or they would have given them up long ago).

Awareness Training

If you've read chapter 10, you'll know I emphasised the importance of the 'pool fence methodology': prevention and education before disciplinary repercussions. However, it doesn't always happen that way. Someone transgresses and we feel obliged to take action, but it highlights a big, gaping hole in cultural knowledge of policy, context, or reasonable contemporary workplace expectations. Thus, the company decides to bring everyone to the same understanding about what is and isn't acceptable behaviour at work. Of course, sometimes this decision is taken out of the company's hands when an external jurisdiction makes a determination about a case that may decree all staff in the organisation need to undergo training.

An increasing number of organisations have online compliance training. Within strict limitations, this can ensure that everyone collides with the key concepts on a regular basis. While the company can then argue that it provides regular training for its people, this does not give its people the same opportunity to challenge, ask questions, and have other colleagues contest their beliefs about what is or isn't reasonable. I have yet to receive any feedback from someone who said that the online compliance training experience was really mindset shifting about things they previously didn't understand or didn't want to accept. In contrast, countless people have told me that the chance to confront biases, workshop case studies, ask the hard questions, be challenged, and be given analogous examples really got them thinking or, even better, was invaluable in shifting their attitudes.

Regardless of how a company chooses to deliver compliance training, it is important that everyone knows their responsibilities and their rights. The training sends a message to all those who may have experienced some unwelcome attention that they have the right to stand up for themselves and seek formal or informal intervention. The training also sends a clear message to any other would-be respondents (those complaint-waiting-to-happen people) that they ought to pull their heads in or risk potential consequences. Of course, it also underscores the rights and the obligations of supervisors and managers who may need reminding about their duty in modelling the right behaviour and acting on the wrong behaviour before people feel the need to lodge internal or external formal complaints, which inevitably take no prisoners. It can also potentially silence the respondent who feels victimised ('Everyone does it. Why was I singled out?') by demonstrating that the same rules apply to everyone and everyone is now accountable!

Parallel Processes (When One Intervention Just Won't Do)

I would think the person responsible for the mass defection of team members in the example given earlier in the chapter was not a prime candidate for coaching but rather for performance management. Then again, it could have been very helpful to actively counsel and warn him whilst simultaneously coaching to give him the best chance to change. There is no reason why the two processes can't happen in tandem so that people know that perpetuating the wrong behaviours places their job in jeopardy while the warning provides a burning platform for change, which may serve as the best motivation for them to commit to the coaching.

Another form of parallel process is to performance manage but give the person the opportunity to move elsewhere in the organisation for a fresh start. Again, if the decision is to keep him or her, then not only must the organisation minimise the chance of further damage to other staff, but a transfer elsewhere under strict supervision and tight behavioural controls may be helpful. What is destructive to culture is to keep passing the problem child around the organisation in the hope that things will change without intervention. Ethically, it is important to advise the receiving branch or department that there have been issues and to ask that their new manager not prejudge the person but rather ensure he or she is managed consistently. I have seen many organisations opt to shunt the person out of one system, only to have the person wreak havoc in another. There is no integrity in shifting the problem elsewhere and then expecting things will right themselves.

Performance management can also be used in combination with psychological support. Some respondents or coaching subjects are genuinely stressed. Problems in their personal lives may have tipped them over the edge. People who are being performance managed for the most legitimate of reasons may become more stressed through the process. My belief is that so long as the decision is to keep them employed, the organisation has an obligation to demostrate care about them, accord them procedural fairness and give them the best chance to turn things around.

Termination and Summary Dismissal

If you have worked hard to promote the values narrative in an organisation, then the vast majority of staff know where they stand. If they believe that management is serious, assuming they want to remain employed, the vast majority will comply. Even those who don't really believe in what the organisation is trying to achieve may adopt a bare minimum acceptable level of behaviour to stave off negative consequences (i.e., their protective drive is activated to minimise the risk of involuntary unemployment).

As long as I can remember, when I've run employee relations training, clients and participant groups have asked some variation on the question, 'Do you believe we should sack those people who refuse to comply?' My short answer is 'yes'. However, a few important points should be considered regarding the legitimacy of the forced termination of employment.

Underperformance

If people have been chronically underperforming, the organisation owes it to them to provide every fair and reasonable chance to succeed, including training, on-the-job coaching, executive or group coaching circles, employee assistance, shadowing, etc. If they can't meet the cut after regular reviews, two warnings and a final interview to explore any possible mitigating circumstances that may have been overlooked, the organisation may regrettably have to terminate. Underperformance may be rare, isolated occurrences, except where it may be reflected in pervasive incompetent leadership with big ramifications for the business. In that case, the impact is vulturesque in proportion, and the powers that be may decide they don't want to keep paying someone a reasonable day's salary if the person is performing in a mediocre fashion.

It is legitimate to sack on performance alone if procedural fairness has been accorded and if the employee has been given all reasonable opportunity to improve and sustain that performance. It is important that any conversation or documentation refer to the requirement to sustain the conduct or performance, as some people will get there and then, when they think the organisation has taken its eyes off the ball, will slip again. The fairest thing to do is let them know the expectation is to get there and stay there!

Dismissal for Misconduct or Serious Misconduct

It is legitimate to sack staff on conduct violations if the punishment fits the crime. Inconsistent application of policies to bring about harsh results for employees will be met predictably with suspicion or may be the subject of grievance proceedings. Procedural fairness or natural justice is an intrinsic value of our employee relations system.

Should any staff member facing the potential for dismissal be given the opportunity to resign? Some of us work under the misguided apprehension that if we ask a person to resign, this automatically staves off a claim of unfair dismissal (because it was a 'resignation'). While I am not a lawyer and you must not take any of this as legal advice, having an employee feel boxed into a corner with a gun to his or her head and five blank shots already discharged may not constitute 'an effective choice' by the employee to depart. That is not to say giving the option to resign isn't a generous offer, but there is no guarantee of immunity from a claim of unfair dismissal if it turns nasty and the employee thinks better of a 'forced' resignation the next day.

The decision to terminate should not be made lightly. While leaders may not share the grisly details of a case with other staff, the staff usually know something of what happened or think they do. As I say to my clients, don't EVER sack anyone just to send a message if the punishment doesn't fit the crime. Recognise that whatever you do or don't do in the situation *does* send a message. If, on the balance of probabilities, the organisation comes to believe a significant 'crime' has been committed (e.g., bullying, sexual harassment, fraud, intention to defraud, corruption, conflict of interest violation, etc.), then be prepared to cut the tangled parachute. Keeping the person in the organisation or allowing the person to resign with his or her dignity intact will send an undesirable message to the rest of the organisation and to external stakeholders.

Case Study — Too Little, Too Late?

A young female patient admitted to a psychiatric hospital for depression was allegedly raped by another patient while an inpatient. She claimed she reported this to a hospital manager, who pressured her to forget about it and never raise it again. This would constitute a corrupt betrayal of mammoth proportions and create even more risk of psychological harm for the victim. Any one of us could understand what a nightmare scenario this would have been for the hospital and why it may have had a desperate desire to keep the incident away from the media, but failing to inform the parents and allegedly pressuring the young woman to keep quiet about it — particularly when she was already so vulnerable — is clearly wrong. The organisation could use privacy grounds to argue it was keen to conceal the identity of the alleged victim for her own sake, but who could argue any justification for asking her to keep it a secret. One would reasonably surmise this was to protect the hospital, not the victim. In any case this distressing story was not kept quiet and made it into the mainstream media.

A number of questions can be asked that demand an organisational response:

- How did the alleged assault happen in the first place? What system or human failings allowed this to occur?

- Had this risk been previously identified? If so, had anything been done about it?

- Did anyone put pressure on the young girl not to report it? If so, was this the decision of one staff member acting alone or not?

- Was the employee's alleged action the result of a directive of someone higher up? If so, were there any consequences for that person in making such a directive?

- How many staff knew of the alleged assault? Did anyone attempt to argue for proper disclosure to the victim's family? What were the results of any plea to do so for the staff member(s)?

- What was done, if anything, to ensure the alleged victim received adequate psychological and other support from the hospital? If nothing, why not?

- Why did the hospital appear to wait until after the alleged victim told her parents to discuss this with them?

- Why did the hospital appear to wait until after the story blew up in the media to admit wrongdoing in the way the incident had been previously managed?

- If the alleged incident occurred as a result of negligence or inadequate supervision by one or more staff members, what, if anything, were the consequences for the staff member(s)?

- If negligence or inadequate supervision were involved, was any action taken against implicated staff members commensurate with the 'crime' and consistent with any action taken previously?

- Has anyone been wrongly made the 'fall guy' or sacrificial lamb for what transpired on the day of the alleged assault and any subsequent decision on how to deal/not deal with such a serious incident?

If such an incident did occur, any action the organisation takes afterward would be likely met with derision by the media, the community, the parents, and the victim. All the hospital could do was to publically admit it didn't handle it well. That is obvious, but the questions above illustrate just how much work is ahead for an organisation if it wants to be serious about such a tragic failing.

Team Healing (Because Time Doesn't Heal All Wounds and Because We May Not Have a Lot of Time)

Despite our best efforts, there will be times that staff still won't make the grade on performance grounds after active performance management, training, coaching, and ongoing feedback sessions. Their employment will be terminated. We may need to heal those left behind, particularly if the exit came on the back of a stressful restructure.

When this happens in a reasonably cohesive team, it's like a child leaving home; the family is breaking up, and a period of adjustment may ensue. I have worked with teams who acknowledged someone was chronically underperforming, but the individual in question may have been a friend and colleague for a long time. Even if the staff understand and accept someone had to go, there can still be accompanying grief.

Our interest here is on vultures, not underperformers, so you may be forgiven for assuming that anyone leaving under ugly circumstances will not be missed. Sometimes this could not be further from the truth. Some of the reasons why a sudden departure for under performance or misconduct can be destabilising for those left are as follows:

- The person is not perceived to have done anything or much wrong (and that is very plausible if confidentiality around the circumstances of the case has been maintained).
- There is a lot of bitterness and anti-management sentiment so that, regardless of what the person may have done wrong, the sacking was deemed unforgiveable.
- The person was very popular or skilled or both, and the loss is considered too high a price to pay.
- Staff may have perceived the person was 'only doing his or her job' and was punished for it (pushing hard on outcomes seen as bullying, for example).
- Others are perpetrating the same or similar behaviours, and punishing one person for this is considered unfair.
- The company may have a history of failing to act on such things in the past, so doing so now is considered extreme.
- Staff may consider, due to unique aspects of the case, that one person is being scapegoated for the many (particularly if they perceive one person is a fall guy for upper management).
- Staff may consider such harsh action may have been to appease government, the board, shareholders, unions, or the media and are bitter about the perceived injustice.
- Staff may consider the removed person had been a staunch advocate for them, and that this person paid the ultimate price (and perhaps that they will now be exposed).
  In the case of a restructure or misconduct, some staff, if implicated on the periphery of what was deemed a sackable offence, may experience survivor guilt.
- Sometimes staff can see that wrongdoing was perpetrated but have an intense dislike for the victim/complainant, and their loyalty lies with the other party regardless of what the alleged perpetrator was claimed to have done.

As noted above, it stands to reason that in cases of serious misconduct, a staff member may be very suddenly dismissed and the spontaneous departure from the team met with shock. In other cases, the perpetrator of wrongdoing may be relocated elsewhere in the organisation, yet staff are still nervous about them being close by. In still others, the team is relieved and more relaxed at an enforced absence for the person under investigation and is then advised the person is returning to the team.

This is similar to any other major change process within a team. It is a naïve manager who thinks that recovery or reintegration is going to happen smoothly without assistance. Individuals may need the Employee Assistance Program, and the team may need some team building, team development, or debriefing (collectively or individually) with the respondent present or separately before that person returns.

Case Study — Victim or Vilified Vulture?

A staff member joined a very enmeshed team some two years before and had found integration difficult. She was older than most members of the team. They found her rigid and pedantic. Staff openly admitted to each other they found her tiresome.

In recent times, a review was initiated and staff were quite stressed. The senior leadership had gone to the trouble of providing good rationale and team support for any changes, but a couple of senior administrators were quite heavy handed with staff, including our complainant, who alleged she was being bullied.

In meeting both respondents after the case, I found them to be very intense, committed women, but I was left in no doubt they could be highly officious when under pressure. They were furious to have had allegations substantiated against them. They had agreed to move out of the area but had kept close personal contact with others still there. The complainant frequently saw them stopping by to pick up staff on her team for lunch. She would get furtive glares and felt intimidated. She said that she was the victim but she was being continually punished because the women she had complained about were the popular ones, and she was expendable.

I was invited to do across-the-board bullying training, but after some tears, flashes of anger, and loaded questions by a number of staff in the training, I suggested some one-on-one debriefings take place. The client agreed to fund a two-hour coaching session with the two respondents, who had left the workgroup and were ensconced elsewhere in the organisation. Staff were also able to request to meet with me if they still had queries or unresolved issues following the training. This was really a chance for them to process what had happened and for me to help them regain some objectivity. There were no surprises when a week later, a whole day was booked with back-to-back appointments.

We had tremendous breakthroughs with the two respondents who had been given very scant information about the findings and did not understand how important it was that the organisation protect the complainant from victimisation. I answered their questions, let them vent, and ensured they understood their obligations. They came round slowly and admitted that they were sometimes heavy handed with other staff. Since they reported to such powerful people in the organisation, it was easy to use that referred power to intimidate and get things done.

The other staff who came to see me were able to admit in a safe environment that they didn't like the complainant and had lost the ability to be objective about who had been the victim and how wrong it was to vilify her now. They also admitted they had been running scared as they worried that if they put a foot wrong – they knew they had been quite nasty – she could complain about them. The respondents agreed they would stop stirring up their friends, and the friends still in the area agreed they needed to focus on getting the job done and working on their relationship with the complainant. As much as anything else, this would be the best protection against the possibility of any further complaints.

When the remaining staff agreed to give the complainant a go, there was a concomitant drop in their fear about being wrongly accused in the future, and they realised that civility and respect towards her was not a sign of disloyalty to those who'd departed the team.

The impact of any one person on an organisation or a team is diffused. The next chapter explores options for the individual staff member who's been attacked by a vulture.

Chapter 13

Coping Strategies for the Victim/Target Dealing with the Lone Vulture

Part of me is always reluctant to label an individual as a lone vulture since many vultures will only have florid symptoms or exhibit behaviours at the extreme end of the continuum in a culture that presses their buttons and enables the worst of themselves to ravage unhindered. I have talked previously about certain stresses or environments that can tip people over the edge, and we have discussed extensively the premise that any individual exists within a system, so damning or pathologising the individual can be a fool's paradise. However, every now and then, you come across someone who's a nightmare!

I will talk about each set of challenging behaviours as dominant behavioural attributes, not clinical diagnoses. You will find it easier and more helpful if I outline and provide some hints for those typical vulturesque behaviours the average employee may struggle to manage rather than clinical symptoms whether found in a leader, a subordinate, or a peer. At the end of the day, it's more important (and professional) to invest in how to deal with them than how to label them. Focussing on countermeasures to challenging behaviours rather than diagnoses also helps you develop some responses to combinations of behaviours you find challenging.

Some fascinating books discuss in detail the various 'Typologies of Toxic' along with some strategies. On bullying, I wholeheartedly recommend psychologist Evelyn Field's *Bully Blocking at Work* for a thorough exposé of what drives bullying and how targets can counteract it or cope with it. Roy Lubit's *Coping with Toxic Managers, Subordinates and Other Difficult People* is helpful in being able to identify different types of toxicity and offers some good countermeasures for handling each. While I am wary of books that have sensationalised sociopathy given that it occurs in a minute percentage of the population, Dr. Martha Stout's book *The Sociopath Next Door* is a *New York Times* bestseller: it is practical, simple, and disturbing.

It goes without saying if all else fails, or if it feels right, escalate issues to senior management and keep knocking on doors until someone listens. Go to HR or the union, and if you think it will work for you, make an external formal complaint. Having said that, please understand you could be waiting a year for a case to be heard, and the pressure will be on you to conciliate a settlement.

Whether you are able to realise justice on your issue, the only person who will go forward with you is you, so my emphasis in this chapter is on you doing the work you need to do to 'heal thyself' so you can move on (inside or outside the company) and flourish.

Below are some of the more common species of vulture you might experience in a workplace and some tips to handle them.

The Bully

The bullies already have a whole chapter dedicated to them, so in brief I refer here to those who threaten, undermine, manipulate, abuse, ridicule, or ostracise. Again, they can only get away with this in a culture that condones, ignores, or actively or tacitly supports or laughs off such behaviour, but they can have a profound effect on others around them who can experience the full weight of the bullying and a sense of betrayal and isolation when others don't jump in to defend them. The bystanders to bullying are often fed by a fundamental need to belong. Better to be on the right side of bullies than the wrong one. If you can't beat them, join them. Bullies often demand loyalty, and those who don't want to stick their heads above the parapet for fear of having them shot off are happy to comply. Worse still, in a sub-conscious need to belong, they can adopt the same norms of behaviour and become that which they would detest if they saw the same thing demonstrated by those outside that system.

What is the worst thing you can do to raise the ire of the bully? The most horrible disloyalty is the crime of being admired or loved more than the bully himself. Be aware too that the bully isn't always the CEO. If the CEO is weak or too nice, the bully steps into the vacuum that's been created. The CEO can remain the humanist, while the bully does the hard stuff and drives the results. This may not be entirely conscious on the part of the 'good cop' CEO, but the CEO perpetuates the system because it works for him or her.

We can call the bully's behaviour; we can get support to prac-tise a courageous conversation. We can use strong nonverbal signals to stop the bully in his or her tracks with a resolute 'I find your behaviour inappropriate or aggressive, and I'm asking you to stop'. If necessary, we can seek help from senior management or HR. Putting in a complaint as a first option is within your rights but potentially creates an adversarial stance as you try to maintain the person is a bully, and the bully tries to justify his or her behaviour and defend the notion that he or she is not a bully.

Telling the bully very early in the piece that the behaviour is unacceptable, is a breach of corporate values, or is personally offensive may nip things in the bud. Even if you're quaking inside, be firm and assertive and fake it until you make it. Do not plead or ask: demand, but not aggressively. Make it clear this behaviour will not be tolerated. Be resolute in your attitude and engage them in confident eye contact.

If you can't confront the scary dude, don't blame yourself, but seek constructive support. Simply avoiding the person may get in the way of the work and is *very* unlikely to effect a change in behaviour. You don't want to give the bully ammunition to argue you are underperforming.

The Narcissist

Narcissists are those who, without becoming overly clinical, really believe the world exists for them (not to be confused with a self-absorbed teenager!). Narcissists are often very entitled and demanding, have poor self-awareness and capacity for empathy, and can become very defensive and aggressive when offered feedback (particularly constructive feedback) because they must protect their perilously inflated ego at all costs. Importantly, they can often have an unhealthy disdain for the rules. They can be consumed with image, appearances, and status, and the fear of a loss of face and a loss of place. This, coupled with their sense of entitlement and self-centeredness, can mean they treat very poorly those they perceive as lower on the totem pole. (I have no doubt they are some of the passengers who treat flight attendants very badly, with or without a few drinks in them.)

You may find these people maddening, low on emotional intelligence, and even offensive in their seeming arrogance. While it is important to set boundaries and not to excuse or accept bad behaviour, they may become vicious if you hold up a mirror to them too readily and try to force them to look inside themselves. Thus, if you have to work with them, try to demonstrate how what you want helps them meet their goals and be prepared to stand up to bad behaviour. Bristling a little or displaying petulance when they have not noticed you at all may be respected. If they decide to like you, hold on to your hat because it's likely to be a wild and exciting ride until they decide they don't need you anymore. Your fall from grace will be swift and hard. Of course, if you want to be authentic and can't stand the thought of being sycophantic with these people, don't go too far the other way. Don't ignore them, box them into a corner, or attempt to name and shame them publicly, as they will resent it big time and may lash out viciously.

The Withholder

Withholders know a lot, but for reasons known only to them, decide it would weaken their position in the organisation if they shared it. This is a very old-fashioned selfish approach to teamwork. It's the make-myself-indispensable routine. In the old days, we were paranoid about people seeing our material or peddling our ideas. Now, many successful people routinely give ideas away free as a way of adding value before someone knocks on their door. It comes from an abundance mentality as opposed to a scarcity mentality. It reflects a generosity of spirit.

Even though withholders are outmoded and to some extent should not be accommodated, my advice is to meet the need. Stroke them authentically about their knowledge and experience and tell them how much you would appreciate if you could seek their advice and share information from time to time. If necessary, inform them you will always honour the source of your ideas and that you won't take credit for their stuff. They may feel obliged to tell you that it doesn't worry them in the slightest, but they may be tacitly relieved. It will also help you if you work within a system possessing of values that actively require staff to work collegiately and engage with others. Mostly, I have found these reluctant sharers are wary. They may have been burnt before and are sick and tired of bright young things coming into their world and failing to pay homage to the past by honouring the vast knowledge and experience of the elders. The more you acknowledge and appreciate, the more likely you are to break down their defences, but it may take a while. Be tenacious. You may hear others ask how you managed to crack so-and-so when everyone else has failed. The short answer often is, you tried harder and respected them for what they bring.

If they don't just withhold knowledge but also actively withhold vital information and maliciously sabotage, you may decide to challenge this behaviour or enlist the help of someone else by providing evidence and expressing concern, not outrage. Be prepared for withholders to tell you that you imagined the whole thing and are paranoid, but if it happens a few times and they seem manipulative or smug about it, you may be dealing with something more sinister than experts wanting to hold on to their expertise.

The Antisocial and Unethical Opportunist (or Sociopath or 'Socialised Psychopath')

These people are principally devoid of conscience and have little desire to be liked or to fit in (even though they may be very charming), so the social niceties associated with affiliation and not wanting to burn bridges are not motivators. Of course, they may be feral to peers or team members but manage to go undetected by senior management unless the metrics of a team in crisis are obvious or someone is brave enough to tell them and hope they are believed as opposed to being perceived as jealous.

Without wanting to overdramatise, they can be dangerous and disarming; they can be very charming and say all the things you want to hear. Befriending you is a means to an end. They are often highly intelligent and can manipulate with ease. The only thing you can rely on them to do is to act in their own best interests, and unless their interests happen to be perfectly aligned with yours, you are best giving them a wide berth.

Further down in the chapter we talk about strategies for the individual dealing with noxious other employees. In dealing with any suspected sociopaths, it is critical that you remain objective about what is going on and don't get sucked in. If you can work alongside them and remain determinedly unaffected, you may be okay. However, you won't want to stand by and see them mess with other people's heads, so one way or another, something may need to be done. True sociopaths, as opposed to moody or angry employees, are impervious to change packaged as training courses or as coaching. In fact, all successful development is likely to do is make them even more skilled at wrapping people around their fingers to get what they want. Whilst not always the case, sociopathy can exist alongside narcissism, grandiosity, the dominance of others, and the potential for other counterproductive workplace behaviour such as fraud and pathological lying.

The Egomaniac

Egomaniacs need and want 'strokes' and recognition all the time. This often comes from a place of insecurity as opposed to the narcissists, who really do believe their own publicity. Egomaniacs' behaviour will be most florid when they are feeling sidelined, marginalised, or ignored. Don't ignore them or work around them, or they will continue to thrust themselves into your orbit.

The Sleaze

Sleazes and harassers could have a whole chapter devoted to describing them and their impact on culture. However, these people are dinosaurs, and we know what happened to the dinosaurs! Some of them are able to build an enclave around themselves and live in a bubble that says 'We're so last century' (and get away with it). But no doubt, sometime soon, the rest of the world will come knocking on their door and barge through it with a battering ram or get on the boat and leave them far behind. If they are directly affecting you, remind them this goes against company values or is just highly inappropriate and distasteful. You may need to say that if this continues, you will have no choice but to submit a complaint, but you would prefer not to have to do that. The other thing that is powerful in line with our 'Is it committed? Is it called? Is it consequenced?' model is to have a colleague who is respected by the group call it. When a close alpha male colleague pulls up a member of the dinosaur tribe and says the person is being sexist and inappropriate, that may carry a lot more weight than if you are left to do it on your own.

The Rigid Control Freak

Control freaks have only one way of doing things. They can be supercritical and authoritarian. We have talked about the qualitative distinction between authoritative and autocratic. The autocratic ones will slowly implode as staff vote with their feet, put in grievances, or refuse to make these people successful. One way of hosing them down is to reassure them you have the same commitment to excellence and check in with them a lot or agree on ways to approach things before you do them. If they keep making up the rules as they go along, remind them about what you agreed and calmly go about meeting the need.

Remember, this is about them, not you (see strategies further on), but you can feed control freaks' anxiety and lack of trust by attempting to go around them. If it is clearly not within the person's purview to be bossing you around (e.g., he or she is your peer), you may need to be assertive and respectfully advise the person that you have it covered and that you find this behaviour intrusive. Alternatively, you could suggest seeing the manager and workshopping the boundaries and interdependencies of the two roles (after lobbying with the manager first).

The Aggressive

Aggressive and explosive people can lose it because they find little or no control when tested. But why, after all those years, might they not aspire to find any? Because it has probably worked for them more often than not. It is human instinct to defend and human instinct to attack to stave off being attacked.

If, for whatever reason, you find yourself at the receiving end of escalated aggression, keep control and calm without patronising.

There is nothing more aggravating to a person who is losing it than to feel judged by someone smug and superior as if to say, 'You're behaving like an idiot, but I'm more mature than that'. Trust me, this is not a time for contempt.

You may decide to tell an aggressive politely that you are both getting upset and that there is no need to get personal. You may ask her respectfully to lower her voice or refrain from profanity. If this doesn't work in the first instance, you may need to emphasise that now doesn't seem like a good time to work though any issues and perhaps it's better to reconvene later. You can put this as a choice and say if the person doesn't lower his or her voice and you can't discuss this more productively (don't say 'rationally'), then you'll have no choice but to come back later, terminate the phone call, etc. Thus, you are putting the choice in the aggressive's hands. You need to strike the balance between being assertive and looking weak or fearful because you want this person to take you seriously. If the aggressive refuses to comply with respectful behaviour, you can either let the person vent and state your point of view when he or she runs out of puff (try to resist the temptation to say 'Are you done yet?'). You will probably only be willing to stand there and listen to a tirade of abuse if you have depersonalised the aggression and do not actually fear for your safety. There is a difference between just being angry or argumentative and on the brink of violence. Experienced police officers can tell the difference very well.

There are four critical points to dealing with uncontrolled aggression:

1. Safety first; worry about the issues later. If you fear for your safety in the moment, get out.

2. Uncontrolled behaviour requires boundaries. Be prepared to set limits on unacceptable behaviour: For example, 'I'm more than happy to discuss this if we are both respectful about it. Right now, I find this conversation unacceptable'.

3. Ask questions (on subject) that force someone to go back up into his head because right now, the person is working from his gut only. Ask questions that make the person *think* rather than *feel*, and he may start to calm down. Call centre operators do this brilliantly when an angry customer rings up:

> '*Okay, sir, to help you, I must ask you a few questions. The letter you refer to, what was the date on the top of it? Can you please read me the reference number? Was there a signature on the bottom of it so I know where to direct your call? Okay, great. I have your details up now. Let's see what we can do for you*'.

4. If you are on the receiving end of a tirade of abuse and you can't get the person to crawl back up into his head, force him to think and make the person feel powerful at the same time by offering a choice. To process the two alternatives being offered, the person has to think. For example, 'Bill, it's obvious you're feeling really frustrated about this. Should we both just relax and talk this through now, or should we go away, get some paperwork together, and come back together later in the day?' or 'Bill, I'm sorry, but I find your language really offensive. Can we talk about this now and be respectful towards each other, or should we abort our discussion and chat tomorrow? I can live with either choice, but not this'. Then shut up and look at him. He then has the effective choice to make and has to live with his decision. (You may have to remind him in a minute's time, but this almost always works).

The Histrionic

Histrionic or emotionally unintelligent individuals wear every challenge and every stress on their sleeve, face, and every aspect of their physiology. They rattle or destabilise others with their flashes of anger, temper tantrums, sulkiness, or moodiness. This may or may not be intentional, but it has an impact nevertheless. People around them usually end up walking on proverbial eggshells.

There are the histrionic, wound-up-tight staff who seek attention and seem to thrive on drama and chaos. The best thing to do with them, if we do not want to establish any pattern, is to be sympathetic without being sucked into the vortex. Remain pleasant and superficial, and if you can, validate the difficulties they're having or the hurt or anger they may be experiencing. They may turn on you if they feel you don't care, and it only shores up their sense of paranoia, mistrust, and sense of isolation. They would probably wish not to feel things as intensely as they do, so trying to blame them for behaviour that they may truly find difficult to regulate is cruel and futile. Trying to stay out of the eye of the storm is advisable for self-preservation. They are usually attuned to the cool, calm, and collected and will work out that you're not going to be much fun and move on to others who feed the drama. However, they live in a highly emotional world and pick up on nonverbal and emotional cues. Therefore, insincerity, disapproval, or disdain will be a beacon to them and may send them even further into anger, rage, or despondency.

Some of us who pride ourselves on being responsive can find it hard not to react and make ourselves emotionally over-available. However, it is neither logical nor appropriate to be a rescuer. Firstly, there is no psychological contract to do so. Secondly, they may not want to be rescued but might be content to grab hold of you and pull you into the eye of the storm!

The Passive-Aggressive Manipulator

These people may divide and conquer as a way of life. Their chief modus operandi is that you can't be friends with everyone, and *your* friend is not *my* friend. Theirs is a divide-and-conquer mentality, much like my school growing up where you belonged to the daggy group, the trendy group, or the in betweeners. They are less likely to throw large rocks and more likely to blow little poison darts. You can sometimes think you imagined the aggression, but while they think they're been subtle, you'll usually pick the behaviour for what it is.

Not all passive-aggressives are unpopular. Some attract quite a following. They can be charming, popular, and fun at parties but sometimes anti-establishment, so hanging with them is hanging out against the organisation. If people are otherwise disenfranchised, bitter, or insecure, this may be a conniving way to display their anger or cynicism. The emotion sitting underneath the behaviour is mostly anger, so calling them and asking what their issue may be could be a good way to get them to take a backward step. Reassuring them you're quite happy to have an open robust discussion but one that doesn't include sideswipes and barbs is preferable. If you can depersonalise the nastiness and not give them a reaction, they may get tired of the sport, but that takes a lot of grace under fire. Even a deliberate surprised look may send a strong nonverbal signal that their behaviour was noticed and is unhelpful without saying anything that may inflame the situation.

There is a difference between letting something go by choice and being too fearful or passive to take someone on. It's mostly a matter of your own mindset and the internal conversation you are having with yourself. Letting go by choice is an empowering strategy. Remaining passive and letting someone else throw darts we don't catch is likely to make us feel weak, vulnerable, or angry with ourselves. Of course, if your team or organisation has a behaviour charter or set of values that include respect, you can remind the other party that comments like those they have made are not in the spirit of the company values, and you would ask that type of thing stops.

Case Study — Marvellous Martha

I recall one woman, Martha, working in manufacturing who was clearly the site character. If you were 'in' with her and she liked you, you were blessed. If she had you in her sights though, watch out. One way or another, she wielded a lot of power, like those feeble frail matriarchs in families in a wheelchair who have total control over what's happening in the family and might whack you on the head with an umbrella when you chew gum or swear.

This particular woman was an EEO nightmare. She swore like a trooper, fixated on people's cultural or religious backgrounds, which seemed to pepper every conversation, and was basically a complaint waiting to happen. If she liked you, she baked for you, minded your pet when you went on holidays, and wanted to see you outside of work hours. If she didn't, she would often monster people behind their backs or attack them verbally when no one was around. Of course, she got away with it because she had a protector. She knew everything going on in the production office and was insulated by the operations manager, whom she had coached when he arrived at the site fifteen years before. He had tremendous loyalty towards her.

I have heard many times that the first outburst by a new staff member behaving in a manner totally at odds with the prevailing culture usually isn't called because people are in shock. But weeks, months, years, or even decades later, why hasn't someone worked out what's going on? This person must surely be Teflon coated by virtue of some contextual variable that affords power or protection. In the case of our complaint waiting to happen, she clearly had a protector at the very top of the organisation. But she was also a font of knowledge, and her expertise would have been hard to replace. Her loyalty and dedication also meant she worked ten to fifteen hours a week more than anyone else, and when she wasn't chewing off peoples' ears and eating them for lunch, she was working hard. It was difficult for the boss to overlook this in a climate where many other staff had a sense of real entitlement, where the work ethic was low, and where if she thought they were slacking, she wouldn't hesitate to call them on it.

So the operations manager fell into line, dazzled by Martha's commitment and hard work. He turned a blind eye and allowed Martha to take control. In his subconscious estimation, on balance, he knew he was never going to tame her, and a company with Martha in it from his point of view was a whole lot better than a company without her. Make no mistake. Martha had a dizzying sense of power as someone whose pay grade was four levels below the operations manager. When I arrived and was introduced to her, she told me in no uncertain terms that what I was there to teach was just a bunch of crap and if I thought I was going to change her, I was sadly mistaken!

Generalised Coping Strategies — Fixing Me First!
Creating Objective Distance or Picking the Pattern

If a person is really immersed in a difficult situation, it's impossible for them to sit outside it and ask how they might respond in another way. They are in reactive mode. The first time something happens it's an incident. The second time it happens, let's call that a trend. The third time it happens, let's call that deeply ingrained patterned behaviour.

Just as the organisation is a system and a team is a system, any one of us interacting on a semi-regular basis with someone else is a system of two people. We can get involved in the 'dance' of that interaction and not even be aware any music is playing.

The first step then to gain some distance is to recognise that some type of pattern of relating has solidified between us. Then we need to see that pattern as not set in concrete. Instead let's visualise it as set in custard and resolve to play it differently.

A Choice to Disrupt the System: Breaking the Pattern

I have had the privilege of working with some pretty intelligent, educated, and successful people in high-rise luxury city buildings with marble and fresh flowers everywhere. But one of the *wisest* men I have met was a blue-collar worker sporting a blue Bonds work singlet, a big beer gut, and some interesting body art. His name was Mick. One time Mick shared with me his definition of ultimate stupidity, which was 'Doing the same thing day after day and expecting that one day we'll get a different result' (Mick obviously knew of Einstein's definition of insanity). In other words, if it ain't working, it's time to do something different as opposed to 'If it ain't working, don't fix it. Let it just keep going for weeks, months, or years!' My advice? Do something — anything — different. But we need to be aware that something is happening with monotonous regularity. We need to raise to conscious awareness that our tap shoes are on and we've been caught in the dance.

My first inclination is to say whatever it was you were doing before that brought you into a collision course with this person, now just *do something different.* But you may want to be more tactical about that. In many situations, actually calling the behaviour respectfully gives the person the benefit of the doubt if she didn't know what she was doing (or not doing) was affecting you. If it continues, you may need to use escalated assertion, reminding the person that you have mentioned this before and you need the person to respect you. You could gently say, 'If it continues, I will have no choice but to … 'and see whether this helps.

I do not recommend you do this with those who are paranoid or ultradefensive, as they will deduce you really are against them and may view your actions not as a necessary consequence of them failing to heed your wishes but as a sign of genuine conspiracy.

Self-Awareness — Where Does That Come from?

How well do we know ourselves? What makes us tick? What sends us into a frenzy? What presses that 'Disc One, Track One' in our internal CD player and trots out the same maladaptive reaction in similar situations?

You may decide you want to read a few self-help books, keep a journal, see a counsellor or a life coach, commit to some therapy, or sit with a wise friend. The journey of getting to know ourselves can be confronting yet rewarding and maybe even necessary. I am not suggesting we have to spend a lot of time looking backward but just some remembering to understand how things that happened back then are affecting us now. Here are a few examples.

- A senior manager I know approached me for coaching because he had a very alpha male, militaristic father who withheld affection and approval and was brutal and demanding. The leader needed to be decisive in his role but didn't want to be harsh. His fear of ending up like his father meant he sometimes hesitated to have difficult conversations and therefore put up with more bad treatment by staff who reported to him than was justified or appropriate.

- A consultant colleague won some work independently and acquiesced to doing the work under the banner of a broker who pushed her to share the profits. She was absolutely unnerved by the hold the broker seemed to have on her until she realised that the sick feeling she had when the broker lectured her about the importance of loyalty and collaborating was the sick feeling she had when she was a little girl and her mother would voice her disapproval at something she did or didn't do. The broker was only fourteen years her senior — not old enough to be her mother, but the parental disapproval shtick was enough to take the consultant back there in a nanosecond.

- A senior executive was shocked at her strong reaction to her 'lazy' kids one night after a hard day at the office. She felt very guilty about the way she lashed out at them. She recalled she'd not been invited to a meeting with senior international guests that morning, had been jokingly asked to fetch coffee for two male executives that afternoon, and then got home to her two teenage boys who pounced on her about what was for dinner as they were starving! This all made perfect sense when we were able to recount the way in which, as an eldest child, she'd been raised by her old-fashioned father who had very high hopes for his sons' careers but thought her duty lay in looking after the family. Chauvinistic double standards and being taken for granted were her push buttons.

- A young graduate started his first job in a high-flying strategy unit for a telco company. An elite footballer before he went back to university, he was accustomed to working hard and doing well. It all came very easily to him. As long as he could remember, people lavished praise on him, and he often won the game off his own boot. Now he was in a very different environment and ostensibly starting from scratch. He was surrounded by more experienced and knowledgeable people than he, and his one big weakness was his prickly defensiveness when anyone tried to given him constructive feedback about ways to improve his work. Those around him began to get annoyed at his abject fear of failure and closed-mindedness to advice from those more experienced.

Some of us may have a little drama queen inside ourselves. Yes, some footballers could dislocate their shoulders mid-game, run over to the sideline, have it popped back in again, run back, and kick a goal, but that's not most of us. On a good day, we are humbled by how fortunate we are. On a bad day, we can decide what we are going through is the worst thing in the world. It may not serve us well to have a 10 out of 10 response to a 3 out of 10 problem. Some of us fall into doing that when we are particularly vulnerable, hormonal, or sleep-deprived. Others of us have an innate proclivity to do so. (My mum is the best storyteller I know because she is a born exaggerator.) I am not suggesting we shouldn't care, and I am certainly not suggesting we should not stand up for good behaviour and great culture, but a proportional response can look very mature and feel less chaotic.

Let's take a leaf out of the book of a doctor in an emergency department. On any given evening, over the top of a cubicle curtain, we are likely to hear someone ask, 'On a scale of 1 to 10, how bad is the pain, with 10 being the worst pain you could imagine and 1 being virtually nothing?' Being able to 'perspective test' what we are experiencing enables us to calibrate our reaction or response against the antecedent event. We are likely to feel far worse and react in ways that don't serve us well if our internal voice is catastrophising what is going on. We don't even want to imagine what 10 out of 10 would be in personal hardship, grief, or loss. It is unlikely that anything going on at work is really that bad unless we are being traumatised, and that will almost always arise in the context of pervasive bullying or altercations involving uncontrolled aggression. Any public aspect to the bad behaviour may magnify the impact of that attention on the recipient. Otherwise, someone else taking credit for our work, a moved deadline, a proposed change, or a terse moment might not really stand up to scrutiny as being the worst thing that could happen to us.

The common denominator to all the keys above is that they demand us to find perspective within ourselves and actively choose how we want to go forward.

If we are really damaged, we may need to take a different tack.

The Damaged and the Distressed

I recall one case I worked on where the employee was very distraught. She was apprehensive to submit a complaint, but she had three close colleagues who told her she would be letting the whole team down if she didn't. Her instinct was to leave and file a complaint on departure or talk about the wrongdoing in an exit interview. They told her she had to be brave for all those other staff members who might come after her if she didn't ensure that justice was done.

My opinion was that it was unfair to have her hang on for the sake of others. Clearly, if no one stands up and says or does anything, the bad behaviour may continue. However, it is not fair to put it on the victim and demand that he or she take the heat for everyone else.

Human beings have a very narrow repertoire of responses to danger or threat. We really only have fight, flight, or flow. In working though our reactions to noxious stimuli, bad work relationships, and toxic workplace culture, I would suggest there are either healthy or unhealthy versions of each. These are illustrated in Table 1.

Table 1

Response	Healthy √	Unhealthy X
Fight	• Fight in the sense of refusing to accept the status quo; resolve to plan and execute a different strategy to improve outcomes for self or both; (e.g., boundary setting or courageous conversation) • Fight in the sense of activating a grievance procedure and asking third parties to determine the whys of the situation.	• Become the behaviour you don't want to see • Fight fire with fire and compromise your reputation and standing • Use their behaviour as an excuse to react. (e.g., 'They made me ... '.) • Could be aggressive, passive-aggressive, or classic 'dirty fighting'.
Flee	• Tactical withdrawal: as an immediate, on-the-spot measure to defuse the situation before it gets out of hand — only designed to provide some time and space to cool down and regroup • Strategic choice (e.g., weight all the pros and cons of staying or going and conclude that all things considered, going will be better for you — walking away with no regrets (leaving the role or the company as a highly intentional, well-thought-out decision).	• Withdraw into self and isolate by adopting an avoidance pattern. • Become the victim and opt not to see choices • Bail instinctively (from the role or the company) without really thinking it through (e.g., the impulsive resignation with a strong likelihood of regret)
Flow	• Genuinely shrug it off and decide you're not going to let the person or the person's behavior or personality affect you (e.g., refuse to take it personally) • Perspective test and decide it really isn't worth the distress • Work to understand where the behaviour comes from and why it has the potential to affect you; observe and acknowledge without judging and reacting.	• Remain traumatised and disempowered • Continue to be exposed to maltreatment

Any or all of the healthy versions are likely to leave us feeling empowered and are legitimate options. Unhealthy versions of the same strategies are more likely to lead to helplessness, despondency, disempowerment, depression, or bitterness. If there is one question I ask clients that they have found most helpful, it is, 'Is the situation (as it exists now) making you feel worse than is necessary for longer than is necessary?' If the answer is yes, the above are the preferred options.

Here are the healthy versions:

- Fight: conceive of a positive strategy and act on it;

- Flee: withdraw either temporarily or permanently but with intention — no guilt, no regrets, and only after considered thought; or

- Flow: achieve genuine peace and mindful calm by objectifying the behaviour, resolving not to take it personally, understanding why it has the potential to affect you if you let it and disassociate from any pain.

Self-Learning, Not Self-Loathing

This is not a book about mindfulness or positive psychology per se, but if you do decide to commit to a journey of self-discovery, the most critical elements of that are not to judge yourself (or the other players for that matter) but rather to focus on how your experiences made you who you are and how you got there. Once you are able to observe those unmet needs surfacing or those vows you made to yourself (e.g., 'I will NEVER let anyone get the better of me again'), it is good to notice that it has arrived and is perched on your shoulders. Then make a conscious choice to notice it and then put it aside. The happiest people in the world are not those who've never had anything bad happen to them. It is those people who've resolved to choose to live a happy life and be 'the boss of their thoughts and actions', regardless of everything that's happened.

A Final Case Study

My daughter walked into a clothes shop a few weeks ago and tried a few things on. We had agreed she would try to find a job now that she was old enough, but she hadn't finished her résumé. The manager apologised for the mess, explaining that the store had just had a new delivery and were drowning in work. Zoe promptly asked whether the store needed any help, and she came home excited as the manager told her to start the next morning. Zoe worked three days straight, so I asked her how it was going. She said everyone was really nice to her except for one young staff member visiting Australia from overseas who had been quite cold and nasty to her on her first couple of days in the shop and kept giving her 'greasers', especially when Zoe made a couple of sales. I asked Zoe what she thought was going on. She said, 'Oh, she was probably insecure that I rocked up and was doing a great job, so I made a real effort with her. I made sure I was polite and friendly even when she was mean, and when I went on a break in the afternoon I came back with some chocolate and offered her some. I just kept reminding myself it wasn't about me. It was the fact that they'd hired an extra person to share her hours. The chocolate seemed to work a treat. Oh, and mum, I think the owner was really relieved I'd found a way to get on with *Tourist Girl'*.

Now that's some emotional intelligence in a fifteen year old!

Final Words

As I said in this book's introduction, people will have had different motivations for reading it. Some of you will have read some case studies and decided your business is in really good shape. Hopefully you've come away with some ideas on how to make your workplace even better. Some of you may now realise you were on the right track all along. Others of you may not have quite grasped the work to be done or the courage you needed to do it until now. It is easy to feel overwhelmed and to use that feeling as a reason to do nothing.

To sit back and do nothing when your people or your business are hurting is in fact a choice in and of itself. Doing something positive is likely to effect a positive change however small for people and for profit. But bringing along others who share your optimism for the future means that together you can achieve so much more. There is nothing that says you have to do it on your own. We can help. So can our colleagues. Listen to the 'elders' inside and outside your organisation and invest in coaching. Have faith in your HR team and let them in but don't expect them to be the sole custodians of culture. You, the business leader will have more direct impact day-by-day than the best trusted advisers.

I am heartened by what I have seen happen so many times in family systems. One different choice, a few well-chosen words, an apology when all you want to do is protect self and blame others, can turn the tide. Every action creates a reaction. Remember the Butterfly Effect that says even the flutter of the wings of a butterfly in the Amazon sparks a chain reaction of events around the world however imperceptible that change may be to the naked eye.

I thank those clients who allowed us to share their stories (de-identified of course). I am always humbled by their willingness to bring us into their boardrooms and their tea rooms and their class rooms to work with their people and trust us firstly, to do no harm and secondly to help them heal. There are actors who say they feel so blessed to be able to do what they do and get paid for it. I feel the same way (but without the limousine or the paparazzi chasing me so it's a mixed blessing).

I wish you every success in your cultural endeavours but as I say to my children a lot — we make our own luck! Be well.

Leanne

Bibliography

Book and Journal References and Recommended Reading

Babiak, P., & Hare, R. (2006). *Snakes in Suits: When Psychopaths go to Work*, NY: Harper.

Bandura, A. (1977). *Social Learning Theory*. NY: General Learning Press.

Beard K.W., & Wolf E.M. (2001) Modification in the proposed diagnostic criteria for Internet addiction. *Cyberpsychol Behav* 4, pp. 377—383.

Bing, S. (1992) *Crazy Bosses*, NY: Morrow.

Brenner, V., & Fox, R.A. (1998) Parental Discipline and Behaviour Problems in Young Children in *the Journal of Genetic Psychology: Research and Theory on Human Development*, 159, (2), pp. 251-256.

Chester, E. (2012). *Restoring Work Ethic: A Leader's Guide to Ending Entitlement and Restoring Pride in the Emerging Workforce*, Texas: Greenleaf.

Clarke, J. (2005) *Working with Monsters*, Random House

Deal, T., and Kennedy, A. (1982, 2000). *The Rites and Rituals of Corporate Life*, NY: Perseus.

Durré, L. (2010). *Surviving the Toxic Workplace*, NY: McGraw-Hill.

Field, E.M. (2010). *Bully Blocking at Work: A Self-Help Guide for Employees and Managers*, Brisbane: Australian Academic Press.

Frost. P.J. (2003). *Toxic Emotions at Work*, Boston: Harvard Business School Press.

Gladwell, M. (2002). *The Tipping Point: How Little Things Can Make a Big Difference*, NY: Little Brown

Goffee, R., & Jones, G. (2006). *Why Should Anyone Be Led By You?* Boston: Harvard Business School Press.

Goldstein, M., & Read, P. (2009). *Games at Work*. San Francisco: Jossey-Bass.

Grant, A. M., & Spence, G.B. (2010). Using Coaching and Positive Psychology to Promote a Flourishing Workforce: A Model of Goal-Striving and Mental Health. In P.A. Linley, S. Harrington and N. Page (Eds.) *Oxford Handbook of Positive Psychology and Work*, pp. 175-188. Oxford: Oxford University Press.

Hare, R. D. (2006). Psychopathy: A clinical and forensic overview in *Psychiatric Clinics of North America*, 29(3), 709-724.

Isaacson, W. (2011) *Steve Jobs*, London: Little Brown

Janus, I. (1982) *Groupthink: Psychological Studies of Policy Decisions and Fiascoes*, Boston: Wadsworth.

Johnson, L., & Philips, B. (2003). *Absolute Honesty*, NY: Amacom.

Kellerman, B. (2004) *Bad Leadership: What it Is, How it Happens, Why it Matters,* Boston: Harvard Business School Press.

Kotter, J. (1996). *Leading Change*, Boston: Harvard Business School Press.

Kotter, J. (2005). *Our Iceberg is Melting*, NY, St Martin's Press.

Kouzes, J., & Pozner, B. (1995) *The Leadership Challenge*. San Francisco: Jossey-Bass.

Kusy, M., & Holloway, E. (2009). *Toxic Workplace!* San Francisco: Jossey-Bass.

Lubit, R.H. (2004). *Coping with Toxic Managers, Subordinates and Other Difficult People*, NJ: FT Press.

Nixon, C. & Chandler, J. (2011) *Fair Cop*, Melbourne: Victory Books.

Schmidt F.L., Ones, D. & Hunter J.E. (1992) Personnel Selection, *Annual Review of Psychology*, *43*, pp. 627-670.

Manning, R., Levine, M. & Collins, A. (2007). The Kitty Genovese murder and the social psychology of helping: The parable of the 38 witnesses. *American Psychologist, 62(6)*, pp. 555-562 on bystander apathy or diffusion of responsibility.

Quinn, J. F., Forsyth, C. J., & Mullen-Quinn, C. (2004). Societal reaction to sex offenders: A review of the myths surrounding their crimes and treatment amenability. *Deviant Behavior*, 25(3), pp. 215-232.

Stafsudd, A. (2006). People are strange when you're a stranger: senior executives select similar successors. *European Management Review, 3(3),* pp. 177-189 for an exposé on homosocial reproduction.

Stout, M. (2005) The Sociopath Next Door: The Ruthless vs. The Rest of Us, NY: Broadway.

Ulrich, D., & Ulrich, W. (2010). *The Why of Work*, NY: McGraw-Hill

Ward, V. (2010). *The Devil's Casino*, NY: John Wiley.

Web References and Articles

News of the World Scandal by Chandrasekhar, I, Wardrop, M. and Trotman, A, at http://www.telegraph.co.uk/news /uknews /phone-hacking/8634176/Phone-hacking-time-line-of-a-scandal.html

Guidelines for Dealing with Patterned Behaviour by Randy Schutt at http://www.vernalproject.org/papers/interper-sonal/DistraughtGuide.pdf first accessed on 11/4/2012.

The link between employee wellbeing and competitive advantage by T. Wright at http://www.k-state.edu/media/mediaguide/bios/wrightbio.html

The 'Masculine' and 'Feminine' Sides of Leadership and Culture: Perception vs. Reality (2005) in Knowledge@ Wharton, see http://knowledge.wharton.upenn.edu /article.cfm?articleid=1287

Walmart's attempt to shift to a values-based culture in The View From the Top, and Bottom on in The Economist, 24/9/2011 first accessed 2/10/2011 at http://www.economist.com/ node/21530171.

World Bank on Corruption at http://www.iadb.org/regions/re2 /consultative_group/groups/transparency_workshop6.htm

The Australia Institute on productivity http://news.ninemsn. com.au/national/283599/australia-the-hardest-working-nation

Quentin Bryce on her assertion that sexual harassment is all about power http://books.google.com.au/books?id= ExkYAQA AIAAJ&q=quentin+bryce+sexual+ harassment+is+all+about+power&dq=quentin+bryce+sexual+har assment+is+all+about+power&hl=en&sa=X&ei=2yqFT6fY KuSPiAf5vZnNBw&ved=0CEMQ6AEwAQ

Dunn-Dyer v ANZ Banking Group Ltd (1997) EOC 92-897

Nexus between innovation culture and high performance culture in Leadership, Culture and Management Practices of High Performing Workplaces in Australia: The High Performing Workplaces Index by Boedker, C., Vidgen,R., Meagher K., Cogin, J., Mouritsen, J. and Runnells, J. M. at Society for Knowledge Economics at http://www.ske. org.au/download/Boedker_Vidgen_ Meagher_Cogin_ Mouritsen_and_Runnalls_2011_High_Performing_Workpla ces_Index_October_6_2011.pdf

B R A S H
consulting ©

Why not use Leanne Faraday-Brash as keynote speaker for your next conference or seminar?

Leanne Faraday-Brash BA Hons MMgmt MAPS FAIM CSP is an organisational psychologist, speaker, executive coach and mediator with 20 years' experience who works with the dysfunctional and toxic right through to the high performing and elite. She is a Certified Speaking Professional (CSP), which is the highest internationally recognised accreditation for professional speakers.

Leanne is an approved media spokesperson with the College of Organisational Psychologists. She has appeared on radio and television and her opinion pieces and expert commentary have been sought in broadsheet and online publications including *The Age, The Australian, The Australian Financial Review, Sydney Morning Herald, In the Black, HR Monthly, AFR Boss, SmartCompany, the Courier Mail* and *National Safety Magazine*.

KEYNOTE PRESENTATIONS

'Vulture Cultures' — on toxic workplace culture and how to shift it

'A Change is as Good as a Holiday — Yeah Right!' —
(customised for change leaders or staff audiences)

'Maximising Me' — on Goal Setting, Motivation and Positive Mindset

Blog: www.leannefaradaybrash.com
Twitter: @faradaybrash
Facebook: Brash Consulting
LinkedIn: Leanne Faraday-Brash

Brash Consulting
PO Box 2389 Caulfield Junction 3161,
Victoria, AUSTRALIA
Tel: +61 3 9505 3070
Fax: +61 3 9532 7696
Email: LFB@vulturecultures.com
Websites: www.vulturecultures.com or
www.brashconsulting.com.au

www.ingramcontent.com/pod-product-compliance
Lightning Source LLC
Chambersburg PA
CBHW070422270326
41926CB00014B/2893